Legal Theory Today
Risks and Legal Theory

C000297181

Legal Theory Today

General Editor

John Gardner, Professor of Jurisprudence, University College, Oxford

TITLES IN THIS SERIES

Law in its Own Right by Henrik Palmer Olsen and Stuart Toddington
Law and Aesthetics by Adam Gearey
Law as a Social Institution by Hamish Ross
Evaluation and Legal Theory by Julie Dickson

Forthcoming titles:

Law after Modernity by Sionaidh Douglas-Scott
Law and Ethics by John Tasioulas
Law and Human Need by John Stanton-Ife

Risks and Legal Theory

Jenny Steele

General Editor: John Gardner

·HART·
PUBLISHING

OXFORD AND PORTLAND OREGON
2004

Hart Publishing
Oxford and Portland, Oregon

Published in North America (US and Canada) by
Hart Publishing
c/o International Specialized Book Services
5804 NE Hassalo Street
Portland, Oregon
97213-3644
USA

Hart Publishing is a specialist legal publisher based in Oxford,
England.
To order further copies of this book or to request a list of other
publications please write to:

Hart Publishing, Salter's Boatyard, Folly Bridge,
Abingdon Road, Oxford OX1 4LB
Telephone: +44 (0)1865 245533 or Fax: +44 (0)1865 794882
e-mail: mail@hartpub.co.uk
WEBSITE: http//:www.hartpub.co.uk

British Library Cataloguing in Publication Data
Data Available
ISBN 1–84113–089–3 (hardback)
1–84113–090–7 (paperback)

Typeset by Hope Services (Abingdon) Ltd.
Printed and bound in Great Britain by
TJ International Ltd, Padstow, Cornwall

Acknowledgements

Work on this short book has been spread over a number of years and interrupted twice for the best possible reasons. Abundant thanks are due to Richard Hart and John Gardner for their patience and encouragement in all of this, and for never appearing to doubt the project. In fact, final completion of the book was significantly assisted by the Arts and Humanities Research Board, who generously funded the final stage under their Research Leave Scheme. I am not sure how else it would have been completed in a reasonable time-scale. I would like to thank the AHRB, and also Andrew Rutherford for his support and encouragement while Dean of the Law Faculty at Southampton; as well as April Boffin and all concerned at Hart Publishing. I am fortunate to have benefited from the patience and support of both publisher and Faculty in the process of completing the book.

Thanks are due to quite a number of other people. Andrew Halpin, Jon Montgomery, and Liz Fisher all generously read late drafts of all or some of the text and I am grateful for their insightful comments. At various other times and in various other ways, I have benefited from the help, time, views and/or support of John Gardner, Celia Wells, Mark Telford, Nick Wikeley, Oren Ben-Dor, Kit Barker, Tim Jewell, and Carol Kilgannon. Some of the ideas in the book were tried out at seminars at the University of Wales, Cardiff, and the University of Westminster, and I would like to thank the participants at those seminars for their contributions to discussion and their influence on the way the ideas unfolded.

Finally, on the home front, many thanks to Adrian for taking his share of the strain, and who must now have tried every available day out in Hampshire for the under 5s. This book is dedicated though to Joseph and Theo. You are the only people in this list

Acknowledgements

who did not exactly help, in fact you have no idea what my day job might be, but you have been two beautiful distractions.

Jenny Steele

Southampton
January 2004

General Editor's Preface

One takes a risk if and only if there is a probability, however small, that one's action will have bad consequences. Since every action carries such a probability, everything we do is risky. This has always been so. It is an aspect of living in the world that has figured prominently in literature and philosophy since the birth of civilisation. This makes the fashionable idea that we are living in 'a risk society' puzzling. In what sense is our society more of a 'risk society' than any other? Are there more risks or greater risks? A cursory survey of the history of life suggests otherwise. Is it that we are more aware of risks? Perhaps.

More obvious to the amateur eye, however, has been the growth of the idea that materialised risk is always someone's fault, in the sense that someone (often an amorphous 'they', the powers-that-be) must have acted unjustifiably (possibly even inexcusably) in taking (or failing to eliminate) risk. Thus when a risk materialises—when the bad consequences come to pass— the question is always instantly asked 'What lessons can be learned?' even where there is nothing to suggest any faulty action by anyone. It never crosses anyone's mind that some- times there is no lesson to be learned. Nobody should change their behaviour. These things—fires in care homes, train crashes, children drowning on school expeditions, homicidal maniacs working in the Health Service—sometimes just happen. And even when they do not just happen, even when someone did make them more likely, it is not always the case that this someone is at fault and has 'lessons to learn'. Sometimes risks are worth taking and we should go on taking them. Children need to be subjected to risk, for example, so that they learn how to live with risk when they grow up. That a few of them drown on school expeditions is the price we must pay. And the only way not to have any more train crashes is not to have any more trains, which one does not need to be a train-lover to regard as preposterous overkill.

The literature about tort law discussed by Jenny Steele in Part II of this book, has as one of its foci the question of when risk-taking is faultless (or reasonable), so that there are no lessons to be learned from the materialisation of the risk and hence no pedagogical purpose in tort damages. Some, mainly in the economic tradition, tend to think that risk-taking needs to be justified (shown to be reasonable) only by pointing to counter-vailing good consequences. Others think, as I tend to think, that this perspective is impoverished. Not only should we not be con-tent to count economic consequences; we should not be content to count consequences full stop. Many valuable activities, from love affairs to business ventures, have their intrinsic value enhanced by their riskiness. Their riskiness counts against them consequentially, but in favour of them non-consequentially. A way of looking at reasonableness that only counts consequences has a deadening effect on our culture by teaching us the mis-guided lesson that we should only think of risk as a negative, and as needing other good consequences to justify it. Of course, some people make an exception for extreme sports. But the problem is nicely demonstrated by the fact that this has come to be thought of as an exception

This is one possible reaction to the economists. A different (but compatible) reaction is represented by Tony Honoré's work. For Honoré, a focus by tort law on the materialisation of risks need not be justified pedagogically, ie by the need for lessons to be learnt. So it need not involve a search for fault, for some unjustified and unexcused risk-taking on the part of the defendant. Two people may take identical risks—one no more justified and no more excused than the other—and yet only the one whose risk materialises commits a tort. The primary impor-tance of the risk is not that it gives one something to justify in court, but that by taking the risk one is gambling on its non-materialisation. If one loses the gamble, one pays. This gives us an interesting new idea about all these people who are constantly asking for lessons to be learned whenever a risk materialises. Their error may not be in thinking that someone has to take the rap when risks materialise. Their error may only be in thinking that this requires fault, and hence that future behaviour should also change as a result. If this is right, we should detach our worries about 'the risk society' from our simultaneous worries about 'compensation culture'. The two represent different morbid social developments: one a morbid preoccupation with 'closure' on the past (compensation, apology, counselling . . .) the other a morbid yearning for an antiseptic risk-free future. The two are unified only by the tendency, which is not a distinctively contemporary tendency, for people to point the finger always at other people and never at themselves.

This contrast and interplay between our forward-looking interest in as yet unmaterialised risks (control and regulation) and our backward-looking interest in materialised risks (attribution and remedy) is the central theme of Jenny Steele's book. Possibly she does not find it all as morbid as I do. Possibly she is more sympathetic to those who want less risk, materialised and unmaterialised, in their lives. But be that as it may she repeatedly brings out the connections and the tensions between the two main ways of concerning oneself with risk. She finds that recent legal theorists in the Anglophone tradition have by and large emphasised the second aspect of the subject. They have been interested especially in which realised risks are 'mine', in the sense that I should bear the ex post cost of their materialisation, either by paying compensation to others or by not being compensated myself. The writers in this vein, who are discussed very thoughtfully and perceptively in Part II of the book, include Honoré, Ripstein and Dworkin. Steele relates their ideas in fascinating ways to some current problems in legal and social policy. At the same time she compares and contrasts this whole body of work with a similarly extensive body of recent sociological and social-theoretical work on risk that is the subject of Part I. Here concerns about attribution and remedy play second-fiddle, by and large, to concerns about ex ante control and regulation. Attribution and remedy are themselves conceived, by and large, as elements of possible regulatory schemes. Here risk is regarded, predominantly, as a collective challenge. At any rate that is a recurrent theme that Steele brings out, contrasting it with the relatively 'individualistic' concerns of the legal theorists in Part II, and the way in which similar 'individualistic' concerns have lately been insinuating themselves into social policy, especially social insurance.

Steele hesitates, and I think rightly, to correlate the forward-looking concerns too closely with the collectivist, and the backward-looking too closely with the individualist. In fact a major objective of the book, and a major triumph, is to reveal how problematic this correlation is, and how much interplay there must be between the superficially incompatible preoccupations of the various writers under scrutiny. For this, as well as its fascinating tour of theoretical issues that currently arise in various important areas of legal and social policy, I am delighted to see Jenny Steele's book in the Legal Theory Today series.

John Gardner

University College, Oxford

Contents

Contents

Part III Environment, Precaution, and Sources of Change

Part IV Conclusion

Part I. Introduction

1
Introduction to Risks and Legal Theory

The short word 'risk' has had to carry a lot of theoretical weight in recent years.[1] I shall be explaining shortly quite how much weight it has sometimes been expected to bear. But first, some comments are needed on the connections between such developments, and the concerns of legal theory.

In general, the appearance of a broadly shared theoretical interest in 'risk' is apt to mislead. Common use of this shared term masks huge variation in what is thought significant about it. In particular, theorists using the term 'risk' are divided in whether the most significant thing about this term is thought to be the threat or uncertainty which it implies, or else (on the contrary) the means of responding to threats and uncertainties which its use brings with it. Consequently, they are divided on the question of whether 'risk' encapsulates the weakness of human decision-makers in the face of hazards and the unknown, thus compromising the power to act; or whether it encapsulates the very opposite, the route by which human beings may achieve control over their own destinies, providing the means to action and decision. I suggest that it is in these debates about action and decision—whether they are thought to be enabled by risk or

[1] Of course, 'risk' also carries heavy expectations in practical scenarios, many of them related to law. The concerns of this book are with the engagement of legal theory with risk; and thus with those other theoretical developments which inform, frame or challenge legal theory in this respect. Some practical legal uses of risk are of course discussed in the course of this book (see for example quantitative risk assessment, in ch 6 below), but there is no attempt to provide general coverage of law's multi-faceted practical engagement with risk.

threatened by risks—that the deeper significance of risk for legal theory has its origins.

At its core, I suggest that legal theory adopts approaches in which risk *enables* decisions and helps to explain the possibility of responsible action. But I also plan to explain some of the stresses which are, or should be, now arising within and around these ideas.

The relationship of law with theory of risk is currently less than obvious. It is clear that many discussions of risk and its broad significance have included comments about the legal system within their ambit.[2] But what has legal theory itself made of the connection? Explicitly, relatively little. But if we focus more closely on some of the most major thoroughfares of legal theory, I will argue that we can make out, however faintly, some important and distinctive routes via which ideas about risk, and especially about its relationship with action and decision-making, are developed and used by legal theorists.

In a sense, I therefore aim to correct the impression that risk 'has not figured prominently' in legal theory.[3] But I aim to do this only in a limited sense. Risk has frequently been not so much a concern, as a *tool* of legal theory. I will suggest that legal theorists often draw upon an intellectual inheritance which also gives rise to studies of statistical regularity and the prediction of specific instances from general data concerned with probability. However, liberal theorists typically eschew a strongly statistical approach, preferring to emphasise those elements of 'risk' which underline the possibilities that it brings for human agency. These aspects of thinking with and about risk have often been neglected. I aim to pursue them further, and to consider the extent to which they retain contemporary relevance, in the course of this book.

Even so, the impression that legal theory is not centrally concerned with risk can only be corrected to a certain extent.

---

[2] Among many examples could be mentioned Beck, Simon, O'Malley, and Ewald, all of whom are introduced in ch 2.

[3] A Giddens, 'Risk and Responsibility' (1999) 62 *Modern Law Review* 1.

Although the language of risk has been used quite extensively in certain aspects of legal theory, and risk has often been used as a device of legal theoretical argument, the source of this device has rarely been analysed in its own right. These 'uses' of the language of risk, and their implied use of an associated intellectual heritage, are of particular interest here. But to see how interesting they are and to begin to test their validity, it is important to be as clear as possible about the broader philosophical implications of discussing problems in these terms. I will therefore indicate some of the broadest contours of risk theory here, before returning to the relationship with law.

Risk Theory More Broadly

In a sense, it is not surprising that 'risk' should be almost universally perceived as important at the present time. At a practical level, methods invoking risk are widespread and often required aspects of much institutional decision-making. There is considerable focus on 'risk assessment', 'risk benefit analysis', and 'risk management' as bureaucratic or financial strategies. But at a theoretical level, some even larger claims have been made for 'risk'. Mastery of 'risk' has been described as the idea that 'defines the boundary between modern times and the past',[4] while risk has also been identified as *the* defining concept of the late modern epoch, taking over the role played by wealth in class societies as we witness the transition to a 'risk society'.[5]

But although there is considerable agreement about the historical origins of the ideas we regard as associated with 'risk', there is much less agreement about the political and philosophical questions which surround the past and present application of those ideas, and their application is typified in widely diverging ways. Furthermore the *implications* of thinking about problems in terms of risk, even more than the methods invoked,

---

[4] P Bernstein, *Against the Gods: the Remarkable Story of Risk* (New York, NY, John Wiley and Sons, 1996) 1.

[5] U Beck, M Ritter (tr), *Risk Society* (London, Sage, 1992).

are subtle and hotly debated. Whenever it is argued that a problem may be resolved by adoption of 'a risk perspective', readers should therefore be wary. It is quite likely that the writer of such a statement is (at best) drawing a veil over the full range of possibilities that such a perspective might imply.

What is Meant by 'Risk'?

In the previous paragraph, I made reference to a group of ideas which is generally accepted as being at the root of 'risk', even if only historically. These are further explored in the first part of the chapter immediately following, which is concerned with risk 'as a decision-making resource'. But despite this common inheritance, a 'shared' meaning of risk can only be stated in the blandest possible terms. In these blandest of terms, the core of risk is a simple state of affairs. That is, **we are faced with a situation of 'risk' when circumstances may (or importantly, may not) turn out in a way that we do not wish for.**[6] Clearly, this falls very far short of being a definition, yet in order to fill it out enough to provide a definition which is adequate from *any* perspective, the universality of the statement would be lost. Whichever way we look at the statement there is something missing; but *what* is missing will vary with point of view.

For example, it would be argued from some disciplinary perspectives that the potential bad outcome must be calculable in terms of probabilities before the scenario can be approached as one of risk. Otherwise, there is a situation of uncertainty at best, and perhaps even of ignorance or indeterminacy.[7] 'Risk' is thus given a particular meaning which is associated with calculability and contrasted with uncertainty. Certain writers, notably Beck, agree that techniques of risk assessment have *historically*

---

[6] The alternative, that things may turn out well, is important. Potential bad outcomes often come between us and something that we wish to achieve. Otherwise they would not be so significant.

[7] For the possible distinctions between risk, uncertainty, ignorance, and indeterminacy, and particularly Brian Wynne's analysis, see below ch 2, pp 32–33.

operated by attaching probabilities to events, yet continue to discuss in terms of 'risk' those contemporary hazards that go beyond probability, and defy calculation with precision. This reflects an increasing colloquial and theoretical understanding of risks as *threats*, rather than statistical probabilities. Adjusting our understanding in this way, the bland statement above would take on quite a different connotation, in which the possibilities are uncontrolled.

But it has also been argued that the most important thing about the situation in which circumstances may or may not turn out a particular way is that these circumstances face a *decision-maker*. On this view, risk is important only because it describes a method for use when we must decide how to act, or how to choose between possibilities.[8] In this book, it is indeed this *association* between risk and decision-making which is of primary importance. After all, if we express our questions about action and potential outcomes in terms of risk, we have begun to impose a structure upon that which is unknown. I emphasise this association because it is important to distinguish this particular sense of risk, which is at the core of my concerns, from the alternative idea that risks are problems which require thoughtful decision-making methods if they are to be resolved. That is why, throughout this book, I will more often refer to 'risk methods', rather than (say) to 'decision-making methods for control of risk'. I am most interested not in risks as problems to be resolved, but in 'risk' as encapsulating a way of approaching problems, and a step on the way to resolving them.

There is considerable overlap, of course, between the ideas that I have distinguished here.[9] But by concentrating on risk as

[8] Giddens, n 3 above, p 8, proposes that '[r]isks only exist when there are decisions to be taken'.

[9] This is illustrated by the discussion in ch 6. The chapter is organised around the idea of risk as a way of structuring our thinking, rather than around the kinds of environmental hazards that need to be resolved; yet of course the material considered concerns attempts to decide how to control or live with these hazards.

a method which structures our efforts at decision-making, rather than on risks as problems to be resolved, we can illuminate certain aspects of legal theory much more successfully. In particular, we can explore the way that legal theory approaches the idea of risk-taking as an essential aspect of human action and thus responsibility (chapter 4); and the way that it employs other aspects of the same idea in order to articulate arguments about distributive justice (chapter 5). Having taken this important step, I suggest that we can and should expand our discussion to take in some of the broader implications of approaching theoretical questions about responsibility and justice in terms of risk. And this means turning our attention to social theory charting the development of ideas about risk, in a variety of ways.

One element of decision-making which particularly affects legal theory deserves to be noted here. This is the question of time. The apparently prospective idea of decision-making informed by ideas of risk becomes more problematic when we turn to the question of responsibility. Luhmann has pointed out that the very idea of risk raises difficult questions concerning the relationship between present and future.[10] Luhmann describes risk assessment as akin to an 'advance confessional' implying that its proper conduct leads to absolution (though when?[11]). For his part, Bernstein says that risk 'puts the future at the service of the present'.[12] But there is no easy way to explain how risk, which on the analysis which follows is used within legal theory as mainly oriented to *enabling* decisions, allows us either to establish or evade responsibility. For example, it has been suggested that responsibility is if anything heightened in late modern conditions,[13] while it has also been argued that the institutions of industrial society have historically weakened the

---

[10] N Luhmann, *Risk: A Sociological Theory* (New York, NY, de Gruyter, 1993).

[11] I will be suggesting, in effect, that present absolution and future forgiveness are very different ideas.

[12] Bernstein, n 4 above, p 1.

[13] Giddens, n 3 above.

idea of responsibility by adhering to the assurances of risk assessment.[14]

The relationship between present decisions and future responsibilities is an issue of some resonance for legal theory as it relates to liability, for example, as well as (perhaps less obviously) for decision-making through regulatory processes. When attaching responsibility, legal theory tends to employ a prospective decision-making model. This model is sometimes imagined to apply retrospectively. In this case, it constructs a moment of decision which may be purely hypothetical, and uses this to draw 'right' conclusions. In some instances, it is claimed that these conclusions can be drawn because there would in the past have been a rational way to decide. In others, the argument rests on the quite different idea that there is a right way to regard our association with the outcomes of our risk-taking. *Both* of these possibilities are approached in terms of 'risk'. Legal theory has in this sense developed specialised uses of risk terminology which, nevertheless, draw deeply on a theoretical heritage concerned with rational action and decision-making. Sometimes the depth of the attachment has just not been noticed. At other times, a wider heritage is drawn on at the author's convenience. Chapter 4 will illustrate this in respect of corrective justice; chapter 5 will provide an example in respect of distributive justice. Finally, it appears that the nature of responsibility and its relationship with decision-making in particular are of growing, not diminishing importance. In chapter 6, this is particularly exemplified through discussion of environmental risk and precaution.

'Contemporary Risks': A Difference in Perception, or in 'Real' Risks?

A problem which is frequently faced in this area is the question of why risk should have become so widely accepted as a key

---

[14] U Beck, 'Industrial Fatalism: Organized Irresponsibility', in U Beck, A Weisz (tr), *Ecological Politics in an Age of Risk*, (Cambridge, Polity Press, 1995).

issue or problem at this particular time, and especially why risk should be promoted by many theorists as *newly* significant, or at least as currently changing in significance. Does this reflect any great change in the 'riskiness' of life in some real sense, it is asked, or does it merely reflect a change in perception, or in response to risk. If the latter, is the general population becoming more *averse* to risk? After all, expanding life expectancies and a well-developed armoury of means to secure personal financial security suggest that the average life in the West is less prone to risk. Is it merely the contrast with these expectations of security that make modern risks appear so daunting?

In some senses, this question is mistaken, at least so far as it implies that greater concern about risk among people in general necessarily suggests greater risk aversion. It might, rather, suggest greater involvement by individuals with the issues of decision-making involved; and greater awareness of the continuing uncertainties. This could be described as greater *sensitivity* to the whole idea of risk and its methods. It does not suggest a less 'stoical' response to potential misfortune, so much as greater awareness of the limits to all attempts to control future circumstances. Possibly, there is also a decline in trust in state institutions; but a decline in trust is not the same phenomenon as a simple disinclination to take risks, or have them taken on one's behalf.

It is true that some social theorists (notably Beck and Giddens) have also urged that the nature of contemporary risks is indeed distinctive, and that it is partly this which has given rise to the new urgency of risks as threats to safety and security. Life expectancy may be higher in the West than at any other time, but they urge that new risks are emerging which are on a different scale.[15] As it happens, we do not have to accept this particular element of their thesis if we are to agree that the handling of risk is becoming more widely experienced as problematic. For

[15] The incident at Chernobyl and the risk of nuclear accident are frequently referred to by Beck in particular. Note also though that 'old-style' risks in the sense of disease and epidemic, for example, are still of enormous importance world-wide.

our present purposes, it is enough to suggest that it is the continued incompleteness of efforts to predict and control, together with the more direct experience of many individuals with risk assessments and the other mechanisms of controlling life 'through' risk, which gives rise to current enhanced preoccupation with risks.

Familiarity with risk and with the evolving methods for decision which it implies does not in the end remove or resolve questions of uncertainty and responsibility. One way or another, and most particularly through the obligation to think 'independently' (but always in terms of risk), people are gaining direct experience of a shortfall between the promise of risk methods, and the continuing exposure to unlooked for outcomes. As part of this change, responsibility for thinking in terms of risk is increasingly passed down to individuals rather than being placed with higher authorities. This enhances awareness of the limits to efforts at control. It is not so much (or at least not only) that there is an expectation of control by others which is increasingly disappointed; more that the responsibility to decide is increasingly placed with individuals, and is noticeably frustrated. These issues are revisited in the second half of chapter 5.

'Risk' and Legal Theory

In this book, I suggest that liberal legal theory employs ideas related to risk and decision-making in order to determine answers to some of its core questions about responsibility, equality and justice. In doing so, legal theory displays a considerable yet limited affinity with some techniques developed through study of statistical probabilities and decision-making method.

Such techniques are often tailored and adapted by legal theorists, so as to be more sensitive to questions of justice and fairness, for example. Furthermore, legal theorists have tended to be selective in their use of the key ideas associated with risk, and have not generally employed statistical probabilities with much enthusiasm. They prefer to adopt those aspects of decision-making method which make a link between individual autonomy

11

and preference on the one hand, and objective or universal standards for responsibility on the other. To these issues, they attach the vocabulary of 'risk'. All of this is explored further in the chapters in Part II below.

Having set up and illustrated a broad 'central case' of liberal theory in respect of risk, I am not however going to suggest that we be satisfied with it. Even within legal theory, it is clear that there are other contenders, or alternative analyses which in their turn draw on very different ideas about risk. These competing ideas are not often cast in terms of their own distinct theoretical heritage, nor clearly compared with one another, although there have been recent attempts to divine the political and philosophical affiliations of different approaches to accident risks and insurance, for example.[16] Here, there is no doubt that changes in the general political climate are affecting the policy prescriptions of those theorists who are influenced by ideas of risk and insurance.[17] The question arises of whether broader changes in theoretical understanding of the nature of risk should also affect such developments.

We must also venture a little further. Otherwise, we may leave legal theory picking up and trying out as solutions ideas which are changing with surprising speed. What are the *broader* implications of expressing ideas about (for example) distributive justice in terms of 'risk' and (perhaps) insurance? What are the challenges and obstacles to the evolution of *environmental* law, which I regard as a special case but one with broad significance? What is the nature of the solutions so far adopted? Here, broad questions about the association of risk with individualism, with collectivism, or with neo-liberal forms of government come into play.

Although I am not suggesting that we should be content with the way that legal theory approaches risks, I am suggesting that

---

[16] See J Stapleton, 'Tort, Insurance and Ideology' (1995) 58 *Modern Law Review* 820; D Howarth, 'Three Forms of Responsibility: On the Relationship Between Tort Law and the Welfare State' (2001) 60 *Cambridge Law Journal* 553.

[17] See P Atiyah, *The Damages Lottery* (Oxford, Hart Publishing, 1997).

its handling of risk is distinctive. Furthermore, that its questions (including especially responsibility questions) retain relevance in the light of some specifically contemporary developments in the problems and issues that are perceived to be concerned with risk.

This book

Chapter 2 collects and distinguishes four broad approaches to risk, which are particularly pertinent for this exploration of legal theory. These also form essential background to the remaining chapters.

The first of these four broad approaches is the decision-making paradigm, which has been described above as being in some senses adopted by legal theory, though it has not generally been embraced in its most 'statistical' forms. Legal theory tends to adopt in particular an 'agent-centred' focus derived from this paradigm. In the first part of Chapter 2, there is therefore some basic introduction to ideas which are generally regarded as inherent to risk techniques. Equally importantly, the tensions within these ideas are pointed out in the course of introducing them. Some of these controversies have become particularly acute in respect of environmental hazards, discussed in chapter 6. Certain of the tensions derive from applying the agent-centred method (with variations) to *social* decision-making.

Second, the chapter goes on to consider a collective or solidarity-based approach to risk and insurance, typified by the work of François Ewald. Here, the technology of risk has an aggregating and classifying effect. Collective solutions are often seen as the only rational solutions to common problems, and lie behind a group of approaches to the problem of accidents, for example. This sort of approach therefore features in chapters 3 and 4 (concerned with liability), but is more directly tested in chapter 5. An aggregating approach is there compared with emerging ideas that link risk with fragmentation and insecurity.

A path from collective solutions implying abdication of personal in favour of collective responsibility, to observed fragmentation and individualisation accompanied by a rather different idea of responsibility, is also discernible in the 'govern-mentality' theories examined as the third group of ideas. These are concerned above all with the use of risk ideas as a *technique* of governance. The adoption of risk techniques here takes on a *strategic* importance. These approaches share a common theo-retical heritage with Ewald, but have developed the study of 'risk' in quite different directions.

Finally, the fourth group of theories takes the idea of 'risk' rather close to hazards. In Beck's particular version, the exis-tence of far-reaching and uncontrolled hazards helps prompt the emergence of a new approach to risk. Beck's approach, and the 'governmentality' theories, enable us to make a broad observa-tion about changes in the nature of risk itself. Both tend to emphasise a combination of *human causes* and *uncertainty* in place of *probability* and *chance*. It was probability and chance which underlay the first two approaches. This change is to some extent the product of new understandings of effects in the world, in which nothing is independent of causes, yet in which out-comes cannot clearly be related to causes either in advance or (often) with hindsight either. This evolution creates far-reaching problems for risk method. It does not cause us to give up on risk as a means of structuring our decisions. But it is likely to change the way that we understand risk. And it also has implications for the likely meaning of responsibility.

After the introduction to different risk perspectives in chapter 2, attention is turned to more legally-defined questions. Chapters 3 and 4 are particularly concerned with liability law, with a focus on liability for accidents and other outcomes. There is an investigation of some resurgent liberal ideas of responsibil-ity for outcomes or effects drawing on risk in chapter 4, but attention is also given to alternative approaches to risk in respect of the same issues, including the role of insurance; of incentives directed to risk-takers; and of new challenges posed by changes in the way that damage is typically caused.

Chapter 5 considers distributive questions, and the influence of risk ideas in elaboration of one liberal theory of just distributions. Dworkin's theory of equality, employing insurance, is compared with Ewald's approach incorporating solidarity, and also measured against the 'third way' theories to which Dworkin himself has made comparisons. But there is also consideration of new challenges emerging from the observation of neo-liberal approaches to insurance and risk—in particular, differentiation and insecurity.

Chapter 6 turns to the regulation of environmental hazards, where emerging problems with risk techniques have been faced in a particularly direct manner. This chapter touches on some of the broadest reasons for declining confidence in probability-based reasoning and in purely 'technical' solutions based on risk, which have been faced quite explicitly in the environmental context. But there are fundamental doubts too about the role of preference and of expectancy value in decision-making about such hazards. Attention is given to some efforts to devise alternative frameworks for the formation of relevant decisions. These range from adapted decision theory, through democratic processes, to reformed institutions of government and associated principles. Finally, attention is paid to the idea of 'precaution' as embodying many of the greatest challenges faced by efforts to define a contemporary method of decision-making in the light of uncertainty.

2
Four Perspectives on Risk

Under the four headings below are grouped those approaches to risk with the greatest significance for our exploration of legal theory.[1] These tend to flow into each other though in their emphases and conclusions they are very different. For example, Ewald's preoccupation with insurance (in 2) is premised upon techniques of statistical observation which were also explored in 1 as essential to the emergence of an idea of risk. Ewald however emphasises statistical know-how and concludes that risk is an essentially and intrinsically 'collective' resource, while much legal theory draws on decision-making ideas to link risk with personal responsibility. The social risk management ideas discussed in 3 bring to the surface dehumanising tendencies in the techniques of risk which are quite at odds with the general direction of the ideas in 1, despite being closely related in some respects. I suggest that all of these have more or less direct significance for legal theory. They therefore form essential background for the discussion in this book.

[1] This is in no sense intended as an exhaustive overview of risk theory, nor even of any aspect of risk theory. Nor is it an overview of all of the approaches to risk which could conceivably be thought relevant to law. Rather, I introduce in this chapter those aspects of the theoretical heritage of risk which are most relevant to the particular contours of legal theory explored in this book. The most notable absence from my direct attention is cultural theorist Mary Douglas, see n 2 below; also M Douglas, *Risk Acceptability According to the Social Sciences* (New York, NY, Russell Sage, 1985); M Douglas, *Risk and Blame: Essays in Cultural Theory* (London, Routledge, 1992). For a general introduction to the social theory literature, including Douglas, see D Lupton, *Risk* (London, Routledge, 1999).

1. Risk as a Decision-Making Resource

The ideas grouped under this heading seek to show how it is possible to take rational action despite lacking certain elements of knowledge. In particular, they suggest that an understanding of uncertainty structured in terms of 'risk' allows us to plan our actions despite not knowing how the future will turn out. An approach using ideas of this sort is extensively applied in contemporary management and regulation, for example. But these ideas are also linked to aspects of law and legal theory because they are compatible with ideas of choice and decision-making and thus with issues of individual agency.

In fact, the decision-making heritage of risk will be seen in subsequent pages to have branched in quite different directions. Both paths are theoretically influential but they are not always clearly recognised as alternatives. On the one hand, there is an impersonal, statistical, and often proudly counter-intuitive sense of risk, which has its origins in the study of probabilities. Sometimes this impersonal approach is unearthed in order to 'demonstrate' true answers or best solutions, and it is also to be seen in the development of 'social physics' and the treatment of social problems through attention to regularity and predictability. 'Social physics' paves the way for a variety of solutions including insurance or risk channelling. On the other hand, the 'decision-making' heritage of risk also influences those approaches which concentrate their attention on an individual decision-maker or agent. Here, the emphasis is on the way that techniques of prediction and rational decision-making can enable individuals to exercise their freedom as active agents even in the face of an uncertain future. No longer governed purely by fate, human beings may reach a decision on rational, or at least identifiable, grounds.

Having clear or rational grounds for a decision is not, however, the same as being able to determine events. Luck will still intervene, and a complex question about the relationship between informed decisions, and unintended consequences, is opened up. It will be seen in later chapters that this relationship can be problematic for theories of outcome responsibility and of corrective and distributive justice; and for questions about the possible bases of environmental decision-making given the recognition of uncertainty. There was a time when this problem could particularly be thought to affect *individual* decision-making. Accordingly, aggregation was the key, since the influence of chance would ensure that outcomes were predictable over a larger group. But increasingly, it is not only individual but also collective decisions which have to be made in the face of the kinds of risks that do not 'even out' over time or with repetition. Thus many of the questions about individual responsibility in prospective decision-making can be transferred to the collective level.

In this section, some space will be devoted to the nature of probability analysis and risk assessment methods. This is not only because such risk 'techniques' and their implications are widely used and sometimes misrepresented, but also because they are in some sense the starting point for all of the other approaches below. Generally speaking, probability analysis is treated as the beginning of the history of risk. Mary Douglas, for example, who considers such approaches to risk to be outdated, nevertheless says that probability theory has provided a 'modern way of thinking'.[2]

The origins of risk in mathematics, statistics, and the discovery of probability are accessibly explored by both Peter Bernstein and Ian Hacking in their respective histories of risk and probability.[3] Bernstein's history is most concerned with developments that have informed finance and economics. Hacking's approach blends history of science and philosophy with an interest in Foucauldian theory. We should be clear that risk and probability, though related, are distinct terms. 'Risk' in its decision making form sometimes depends upon a formal

[2] M Douglas, 'Risk as a Forensic Resource' (1990) 119 (4) *Daedalus* 1.

[3] P Bernstein, *Against the Gods: The Remarkable Story of Risk* (New York, NY, John Wiley and Sons, 1996); I Hacking, *The Emergence of Probability* (Cambridge, CUP, 1975); I Hacking, *The Taming of Chance* (Cambridge, CUP, 1990).

computation of probability,[4] and in all cases it requires some assessment of likelihood. So risk in this sense is either strongly or weakly dependent on judgments of probability. 'Probability' on the other hand can be used for many purposes including analysis of past events (X 'probably' caused Y), not all of which involve risk assessments. Risk assessment generally concerns the future, though its use to judge or debate the past has already been mentioned here.

The understandings of risk in its decision-making sense are broadly positive: to understand a problem in terms of risk is to create an opportunity for action, and to remove the causes of indecision. However, we should be clear that merely expressing a problem in terms of risk and probability does not in principle lead us to 'discover' what to do. Rather, the analysis in terms of risk should enable us to make a *choice*, on the basis of structured information (some of which is lacking). This simple limitation is often forgotten in the heat of argument. In some instances, arguments are set out which seek to 'demonstrate' the right course of action using risk techniques or pure statistical observation.[5] Acceptance of such arguments will depend either upon accepting certain hidden value judgments,[6] or upon agreeing certain principles, for example relating to 'dominance', 'maximin', or the avoidance of catastrophe.

Risk techniques neither reveal nor determine the future, but they seek to enable us to choose, and provide a basis on which to do so. Seen in this positive yet limited sense, risk gives us what we need in order to make decisions. But this means only that it *removes indecision*, not that it puts the decision beyond reproach or regret. The connection between prospective decision and retrospective judgment or regret continues to be

[4] Some technical uses insist that risk must be calculable in terms of probabilities: see for example N Barr, *The Welfare State as Piggy Bank* (Oxford, OUP, 2001).

[5] See the exploration of Quantitative Risk Assessment and its apparent suppositions, in ch 6 below.

[6] For example, that the loss of one set of lives is exactly equivalent to the loss of the same number of other lives.

problematic, and indeed it is arguable that greater consciousness of the limitations of risk as a method, and greater focus on the outcomes of action and the elusiveness of the future, are currently undermining the advantages which were associated with risk. Increasingly, risk brings implications of responsibility and choice. It does not uncover solutions through technical application of probabilistic method.

Probability: Frequency or Belief

Two senses in which decisions about risk are necessarily 'subjective' are explored below in terms of 'the value element'. But risk analyses generally depend upon assessments of probability, and there are sometimes arguments about whether probability assessments *themselves* should be described as 'objective' or 'subjective'. Alternative (and possibly less confusing) terminology would refer instead to 'frequency statements' (sometimes referred to as 'objective') or 'belief statements' (sometimes called 'subjective' or 'epistemic').

Some theorists have argued that all probability statements are frequency statements, others that probability statements as a whole are 'only' propositions, or statements of belief. There is a more common view, that both sorts of probability statement exist. If so, the boundary between them has proved hard to define, although focal cases are clearer. The issue is of broad significance for the general nature of decision-making based on risk.

Historically, the techniques of risk were related to observation of events and especially *regularities*. Early studies in probability focused upon random events in games of chance: roulette wheels, cards, dice, the tossing of coins. Truly random events of this sort became understood as highly predictable, over a large enough sample. According to Ian Hacking however, emerging ideas about probability were quickly applied to two rather different sets of problems, and probability has always had two aspects.[7] The first concerns statistical analysis derived from

---

[7] I Hacking, *The Emergence of Probability* (Cambridge, CUP, 1975) chs 2 and 8.

observation, allowing comprehension of 'chance occurrences' and the discovery of 'laws' with which these occurrences seem to conform. This aspect of probability could be described as allowing us to know what to expect, based on frequencies. It allows us to make up for absent knowledge by understanding the nature of 'chance', because chance occurrences are discovered to conform to certain patterns. The other is a 'decision-theoretic' aspect. This is distinct partly because it allows for the extension of probability theory to situations where something is unknown, but the unknown factor is no mere matter of chance.

Hacking illustrates this duality using two famous seventeenth century 'discoveries' attributed to Pascal. The first was concerned with the prediction of chance events. Here, Pascal corresponded with Fermat concerning a long-standing puzzle, of how to allocate fair shares between two participants in a game of chance, when their game was incomplete.[8] The solution to this puzzle was reached by setting out what we should expect to be the pattern of hypothetical future games: we may then divide the stakes accordingly. This is a question of frequencies, assuming the game to be truly governed by chance. However, it was also perceived to be a question of fairness, and the just distribution of stakes.

The second is the 'decision-theoretic' issue of how to behave, and what to believe, given that we lack proof of the existence of God. The solution to this is well known as 'Pascal's wager'.[9] The details of Pascal's argument have been thoroughly criticised (and sometimes supported),[10] but it is the general question behind the wager which matters now. What belief is rational,

[8] 'The problem of the points': see also Bernstein, n 3 above, pp 63–68.

[9] The whole question of choosing 'what to believe' makes sense only if one accepts Pascal's view that one can choose a course of action which will encourage the development of belief-or, one may do the opposite.

[10] For criticisms, see eg B Williams, 'Rawls and Pascal's Wager', in B Williams, *Moral Luck* (Cambridge, CUP, 1981), and his references there. Pascal's method is defended by I Hacking, *The Emergence of Probability* (Cambridge, CUP, 1975) ch 8, although he accepts that the simple binary opposition adopted (God exists, or does not) strikes most people now as wrong, given the existence of many different incompatible theologies.

and what action logical, given the relevant absence of knowledge? Hacking observes that this is quite distinct from the question of 'what to expect', and relates to 'what to believe' or 'what to do', given different potential outcomes. It is an exercise in conjecture, transferring the structure of reasoning about games of chance, to 'non-chance occurrences'.

It will be noticed that even in the absence of frequencies, the method of the argument is to attempt a *reasoned* account of why one should act in a particular way. Pascal's wager does not simply represent a gambler's musings on whether to place a bet: it is designed to persuade and, in a sense, to 'prove' what the right course of action is. The wager takes us into the realms of decision-making theory and inductive logic, and depends (probably) on an idea about 'dominance'—on the awfulness of getting the wager wrong in one particular way.

'Frequency' and 'belief' senses of probability can also be illustrated in a rather different way. First, imagine that a scientist asserts 'with 90% certainty' that a giant asteroid wiped out the dinosaurs.[11] The scientist's *quantification* of certainty at 90% is a statement about her degree of belief that the proposition is true, and not about relative frequencies. In a sense, it is misleading to describe this statement as 'subjective', because it may well rest on testable evidence of a 'non-frequency' type. Nevertheless, in the terminology above that is how it would be described.

By contrast, an insurance company will predict how likely I am to crash my car in a given year, dependent upon categorisation of me into a group, and observation of frequencies of crashes in that group in previous years.[12] My probability of a car crash, as determined by the insurer, is a statement in terms of *frequency*. It would be referred to as 'objective'. Yet the chance of my crashing is not a truly random occurrence. The insurance company tries to deal with this by discriminating between

[11] This example is taken from I Hacking, *An Introduction to Probability and Inductive Logic* (Cambridge, CUP, 2001) 128–30. The statement is one of probability, but not of risk: it is entirely backward-looking.

[12] Their quantification is a risk statement: it is forward-looking.

applicants on various grounds: age, gender, experience, type of car. In principle, extra non-frequency elements of knowledge about my personal likelihood of a crash could have been obtained: am I a safe driver, or not? But conventionally, it is assumed that practicality dictates that only easily obtained information may be used by insurers. It must also be easy to assimilate in an actuarial fashion.

Though crashes are not truly random occurrences, the point is simply that they *can* be treated almost as though they were. The estimation of my risk in terms of frequency, and the construction of the groups with which I am assessed, represent a choice on the part of insurers, guided by practicality and experience. This will be quite important when assessing insurance and its relationships with justice (see Chapters 3 and 5 below). But it also helps to explain why insurance is not a model for all risk-taking. Typically, the insurer's methods depend upon aggregation, and experience. Some significant risks are non-random, less susceptible to aggregation, and untested by experience.

The Value Element

There are many evaluative elements in risk assessment. For example, how do we assess 'evidence' for a risk, and what counts as 'evidence' anyway? But in any argument about the uses of risk, it should be remembered that *all* risk assessment can be said to be evaluative to the core. Apart from the divergence of view over what probability is, two crucial aspects of the evaluative element have long been recognised. The first is the attachment of value to possible outcomes; the other is 'risk-aversion'. Given the on-going debate about use of risk assessment techniques, both for the purposes of regulation and in normative theory, it is important to be clear about these value elements.

To one extent or another, all risk assessments involve the calculation not just of odds, but of the value of those odds. At its simplest, this means combining the likelihood or probability of an adverse outcome, with the 'cost' of that outcome. Cost, however, is a subjective matter. If the bad outcome is that we lose a certain amount of money, or are liable for a certain amount of damages, then it appears relatively easy to attach a figure to the potential loss. These are the least problematic cases, but they are still not problem-free. The value of money to X depends very much on what other resources X has, for example. To recognise this is to introduce an important distinction, between **mathematical value** (which is the same for everyone), and **utility**. The money value of a risk may be calculable, yet this will not reveal the utility value of the risk. The distinction between mathematical value and utility is further explored immediately below. But if the possible losses are *not* purely financial, it is much harder to attach the right 'value' in any calculable form at all. This has clear implications for the use of quantitative or numerical risk assessment in respect of many matters including health and safety and risks to the environment.

Once a 'value' has been attached to the potential losses, risk assessment methodology would propose that we set that 'value' against the potential *gains* from the course of action being contemplated. Risk assessment is usually carried out in preparation for the choice between different possibilities, even if the choice is only whether to take a certain gamble, or not. To decide whether to take that gamble, we need to compare possible gains with possible losses, including both dimensions of probability and value. Together, these are used to arrive at **'expectancy value'**, which may be positive or negative. Use of expectancy values is least problematic in situations where there is one person making a decision for herself concerning risks and benefits to her alone. It becomes more difficult to define the proper role of this concept in a situation where one person decides whether to impose risks on another, or a group decides what risks will be run by the group as a whole (or even by some other group, such as a future generation). But at any level, it should always be remembered that any assessment of risks, no matter what the context, *should depend on the ascription of value, not just probabilities, to potential outcomes.*

According to Bernstein, it was Daniel Bernoulli who in 1738 took the important step of considering games of chance in terms of 'utility' to the players, rather than in terms of impersonal odds.[13] What this move added was a focus on particular risk-takers. It also took seriously the idea of personal values as opposed to mathematical or 'objective' values. Each player, according to Bernoulli, would have their own set of values, which would influence their decisions in respect of which gambles to take. However, Bernoulli also proposed that there would be some regularity in the way that individuals responded to particular risks and opportunities. In particular, their desire to undertake risky opportunities would wane the richer they became. Bernoulli introduced a focus on subjectivity, but also proposed a degree of uniformity or predictability in the response to risks. This latter insight is still in active use as the idea of 'declining marginal utility'.[14]

But this is only one way of expressing Bernoulli's contribution. To put it another way, his insights propose that *decisions* about which risk to take are affected by the dimension of 'risk aversion'. It is true that diminishing marginal utility gives a reason for risk aversion in some circumstances: if I am less eager to add to my wealth, I will be less tolerant of gambles bringing potential losses. But risk aversion is a rather broader concept than this, which adds necessary elements of subjectivity to any decision about which risks to run. It also explains different attitudes to 'being at risk'. Bernstein explains that we can all agree, if properly informed, about the length of the odds against being struck by lightning or of being involved in a plane crash, yet still display very different responses to the experience of an electric storm or even of flying. These different responses do not depend upon mistakes. As Bernstein puts it, Bernoulli's key insight is that 'gut rules the measurement'—and that it does so without any failure of logic.[15]

So far as expectancy value is concerned, there is more than one way of expressing its relationship with risk aversion. One way of

[13] Bernstein, n 3 above, pp 99–115.

[14] See for example the discussion of Coleman's contractual solution to products liability questions, in ch 3 below.

[15] Bernstein, n 3 above, p 105.

expressing this relationship is to say that expectancy value is not the whole story. To say this is usually to assume that expectancy value has a mathematical form, so that the dimension of preference in respect of risk-taking adds a quite different dimension. Risk aversion is a separate idea which works upon the basic statement of expectancy value. On this basis, we may decide not to take a risk despite its positive expectancy value. We do not think it worthwhile. The alternative is that statements of expectancy value could be adjusted in the light of risk aversion, perhaps by expressing them in terms of 'utiles' rather than in terms of simple money value. The important thing here is that this exercise would add extra complexity and controversy to the process of expressing expectancy value. In general, it would imply that a course of action or risk-taking option would have different expectancy values for different individuals. Statements of expectancy value for societal decision-making set on this approach would be inherently controversial and must be preceded by some sort of value-setting process which takes into account risk aversion. On both accounts, the role of risk aversion unavoidably adds extra elements of subjectivity to the decision whether to take a particular course of action involving risk, but it does so at a different stage.

Perhaps the most familiar example of risk aversion in practice is insurance. Commercial (as opposed to social) insurance is dependent on risk aversion among consumers, except where it is required by law or as a condition of getting something else (such as a mortgage). Commercial insurance policies do not have positive expectancy value to consumers. But this does not mean that the purchaser of insurance has been duped. Simply, it is considered better to accept a negative but moderate-to-bearable *mathematical* expectancy value (spend money on the insurance premium even though it is likely we will make no claim), than to take the chance of a large loss after which we might not recover an existing or even a tolerable lifestyle. Logic is not the only determinant of consumer behaviour, but the point is that even in logic, there are necessary issues of risk aversion which are relevant to decisions involving risk. In principle, logic alone *cannot* tell us which decision to make.

I do not mean to conclude that there is no way (beyond the search for logical flaws) of judging risk decisions, nor that preferences are beyond comment as a matter of reason. This is important, and it may help to consider how we would react to somebody who is not, as it turns out, risk averse, and therefore does not purchase basic insurance to cover disability despite enjoying ample income. Would we describe such a decision not to protect oneself through insurance as *irrational*? If we establish that the decision-maker fully understands the risks, we may conclude that the decision is not based on faulty logic. It would be hard to justify calling it 'irrational'. Would we nevertheless describe her decision as *unreasonable*? Perhaps. But if so, is this because of the burden she may impose on others (we do not think her behaviour *responsible*, or acceptable)? Or, because we cannot imagine anyone else sharing her view (she defies expectation, or is not *normal*)? Questions like these are important to consideration of reasonable and rational choices and their use in legal theory. But they are equally resonant of further obligations upon individuals, to reason and act in a responsible and security-conscious manner, as members of 'risk society'.

Because the issue of rational choices under uncertainty is so important to legal theory, it should be mentioned that the trend of more recent studies of risk aversion and of psychological responses to risk suggest that some existing assumptions about risk-taking behaviour are mistaken. People do not exhibit behaviour conforming with the rational choice theory of risk-taking and especially the predicted form of risk aversion. In fact, these recent theories tend still to find regularities in people's responses to risk. For example, it is proposed that instead of risk aversion, we seem to exhibit something like *'loss* aversion'. We are much more willing to take risks with potential gains than with potential losses, and prefer to risk what we could have, than what we have already got.[16] This means that people's responses can be easily manipulated by putting the same question to them in

[16] This is drawn from Kahnemann and Tversky's 'prospect theory', which is discussed in ch 6 below.

different ways: the findings can be understood as exposing popular irrationality. But the existence of previously unexpected forms of discrimination among risks on the part of 'most people' is important information. What we make of this information is linked, once again, with issues surrounding reasonableness and rationality. In chapter 6, this type of research is also treated as providing a bridge between decision theory, and the broader questions surrounding social decision-making.

Liberalism, risk and decision-making resources

In part 2 of this book, I suggest that risk in the decision-making sense is deeply attractive to liberal legal theory partly because it hints at the possibility of a 'planned life'. Individuals who have mastered the idea of risk can act autonomously, not in the sense that they are free from one another or free from control, but in the sense that they are free from the paralysis of subjection to fate. Perhaps, they are free *to decide.* As Bernstein puts it, risk brings the notion that 'the future is more than a whim of the gods and that men and women are not passive before nature'. In chapter 1, we also noted his further suggestion, that risk 'puts the future at the service of the present'. It may do so, but only in a certain sense. In making a decision according to the methods of risk, we use an image of the future, and employ this image to enable us to meet our own goals for the time being. But we cannot determine that future. Unless with the help of repeat performances and the 'law of large numbers', we cannot say how things will turn out for us. And there are many situations in which the law of large numbers is simply inapplicable, or cannot be expected to hold.

Risk in its positive, opportunity-creating sense is compatible with the richer liberal ideal of the autonomous individual who seeks to maximise his wellbeing through pursuit of a good life. It is also linked with profit-making activity. Small wonder that decision-making ideas drawing on risk have been extensively used within liberal theories of justice, for example.

Risk in its decision-making sense has also been presented as linked with human freedom at the deepest historical level.

29

Bernstein for example takes the view that advances in probability theory became possible only when a certain view of humanity became accepted. That is, he argues that the discovery of probability had to wait for the Enlightenment period because until that time, it was thought that 'fate' or the gods were the only determinants of good or bad luck. The arrival of a concept of risk marks a real stride forward into freedom, because it allows us to choose our actions, and in *some* sense our destiny, in the light of reliable information, even in the absence of knowledge. This was (literally) unthinkable until a certain historical point.[17] But Bernstein also takes his story of risk to the point where we ourselves constitute a paradox. The failure of human beings to conform to the rules of logic in their own behaviour, and the extent to which human intervention weakens the effects of chance, simultaneously undermines our efforts at control, while vindicating human freedom. It weakens the suspicion of determinism, which has haunted approaches based on observed regularity in human affairs. But it also removes part of the security that risk 'methods' provided. The connections between risk and human freedom are therefore complex, but even within a decision-making paradigm, the way that risks are understood has altered significantly in recent years.

The Undermining of Chance and Probability

So far as both probability and decision-theory provide technical or methodological ways of determining what to do in the face of uncertainty, which are also philosophically appealing from a liberal perspective, it is important to note some recent trends which threaten to undermine these approaches.

The first has already been set out: that the influence of human decisions on events means that fewer events are to be treated as true 'chance' occurrences. Secondly, continuing concentration on the subject of risk means that increasingly, it is risk itself

---

[17] Note, though, that Hacking emphasises that regularity–at the core of probability as it emerged–was thought by some of the pioneers of probability to illustrate that the world could only have been ordered by a divine intelligence.

(rather than material outcomes) which becomes the focus of attention. Because risk, as a method, is in some sense designed to relieve actors of intolerable burdens, or to create a point in time at which a decision is at least possible, the shift in interest to risk *per se* is itself capable of undermining the point of risk, which is to enable decisions to be made. Risks and outcomes become blurred. Thirdly, natural and actuarial science also move on. In particular, it is increasingly recognised not only that establishing the links between actions and effects is frequently a matter of probabilities in itself, even after the event; but also that the potential outcomes of action are difficult to itemise in full, and will often only be recognised with hindsight. The world, as Beck puts it, has become a laboratory.[18] To say this is to recognise that outcomes are partly of our making, and subject to our influence, even if the causal links are diffuse and uncertain. Further, experimentation often precedes research into likely effects. But, we may add, life is not, after all, a lottery, dictated by the laws of impersonal chance and amenable to control through the understanding of statistical regularity.

Risk, Uncertainty, Ignorance and Indeterminacy

It is worth pausing here to consider some potential problems with terminology relating to 'risk'. Risk is sometimes treated as synonymous with uncertainty, or as providing a method applicable precisely to uncertain situations. This is not merely a 'careless' habit. For example, decision theory often refers to the central idea of a gamble, in a game of true chance, as a 'decision under uncertainty', meaning simply that the decision-maker does not know how things will turn out. This is also treated as the paradigm case of 'risk'. Other uses of the terminology of risk and uncertainty however are more choosy, insisting that only if the likelihood of an outcome can properly be expressed *in terms of probabilities* should the term 'risk' be used. Otherwise, it is relevant only to talk in terms of 'uncertainty'.

[18] U Beck, *Ecological Politics in an Age of Risk* (Cambridge, Polity Press, 1995) 122–25.

But it should be recalled that according to Hacking, probability ideas were quickly applied even to circumstances which could not truly be captured in terms of statistical regularity (including, most obviously, the existence of God). Thus right from the start, probability itself has been assigned to situations which are beyond the clear parameters of known regularities. It is true that cases where probabilities are assigned on bases other than the laws of chance or of actuarial experience raise particular problems, and that the *source* of probability judgments should always be questioned: this is discussed in respect of quantitative risk assessment in chapter 6. But I do not think it would be possible to discuss the influence of risk ideas in law sufficiently fruitfully if only the purest of statistically-based 'probability' statements were included in the definition of risk.

Even so, it is important to be aware that there are forms of uncertainty which threaten to surpass at least existing methods of risk assessment, and possibly could be argued to be outside the reach of 'risk'. At this stage, it is perhaps most useful to refer to Brian Wynne's well-known 'taxonomy of uncertainty', although he defines risk and uncertainty themselves in stricter terms than I have proposed above.[19]

According to Wynne, **risk** is a term properly used where system behaviour is known, and outcomes can be assigned a probabilistic value. Wynne probably has in mind here that there should be a sound actuarial or statistical basis for the assignment of such probabilities, which should not be based purely on conjecture or supposition. **Uncertainty** should be referred to when important system parameters are known, but not the probability distributions. The division between these two seems to turn then on what is treated as 'known'. More importantly for the present, Wynne includes two further and more 'uncertain' forms of not

[19] B Wynne, 'Uncertainty and Environmental Learning: Reconceiving Science and Policy in the Preventative Paradigm' (1992) 2(2) *Global Environmental Change* 111; for discussion see SR Dovers and JW Handmer, 'Ignorance, Sustainability, and the Precautionary Principle: Towards an Analytical Framework', in R Harding and E Fisher (eds), *Perspectives on the Precautionary Principle* (Sydney, Federation Press, 1999).

knowing *beyond* risk and uncertainty. These are respectively **ignorance**, where 'what is not known is not known', and **indeterminacy**, where causal chains, networks, and processes defy prediction. Clearly, these last two forms of uncertainty challenge the very construction of decision-making models. Arguably, complex and interrelated risks like many of those affecting ecological systems, often fall within the definitions both of ignorance, and of indeterminacy. Thus debates in this field surround the very asking of 'risk' questions, rather than just the answers proposed. According to Ian Hacking, the growing *recognition* that we are ignorant, and especially that we are ignorant of the way that our actions will interact with other factors, means that we are increasingly 'culpable' (we might prefer to say 'responsible') even in cases of ignorance.[20] Ignorance loses its innocence, as awareness of the limits to knowledge grows.

In summary, the recognition of stronger forms of uncertainty does not take us outside the discussion of issues which have been approached in terms of risk in legal theory. But it does pose extra challenges to the solutions reached to date, and if anything places *extra* emphasis on the need to explore responsibility for effects, and the very nature of decisions.

2. Risk and Collective Technology

The second broad perspective on risk overlaps with the first, since it places the origins of risk in statistical enquiry. From here however, it takes a different course. François Ewald argues that 'risk' is nothing but a term derived from the practice of insurance, and that its only precise (as opposed to colloquial) meaning relates to insurance terminology.[21] This approach also has broad overlaps with the other Foucauldian approaches

[20] I Hacking, 'Culpable Ignorance of Interference Effects' in D MacLean (ed), *Values at Risk* (Totowa, Rowman and Allenheld, 1986).

[21] F Ewald, 'Insurance and Risk' in G Burchell, C Gordon, and P Miller (eds), *The Foucault Effect: Studies in Governmentality* (Chicago, IL, University of Chicago Press, 1991) 197–210. See also F Ewald, *L'Etat Providence* (Paris, Grasset, 1986).

considered as a third perspective, below. But because Ewald makes distinctive, positive philosophical claims for the development of insurance technology, and because the influence of these can be felt through the next few chapters, I have chosen to explore his theory separately.

In Ewald's usage, 'risk' is (or was)[22] not a danger or threat, but a technical means of ordering certain possibilities and their occurrence to certain individuals. Insurance depends upon classification of individuals and events into 'risk categories', based on actuarial information. People, things, and events are grouped, and only in this way are risks *created*. Risk could not exist without classification. This specifically emphasises the statistical and aggregating aspects of the discussion in (a) above, and identifies risk with these alone. Thus, the decisive move made in the instigation of wide-spread insurance is the application of statistical laws to human affairs, rather than just to games of chance or true random occurrences. The application of such techniques does not in principle deny the freedom of action of the population: it does not amount to an argument that human acts are *truly* random. Nevertheless, the application of statistical methods to human affairs—or 'social physics'—is argued by Ewald to have had significant philosophical implications.

According to Ewald, insurance creates 'epistemological transformations', leading to a fully-fledged 'philosophy of risk'. I have hinted that in liberal theory, the decision-making ideas described above are used with a focus on individual decision-making. Their model is the individual gambler who must structure his decisions through information and techniques derived from probability. By contrast, Ewald argues that 'risk' *is collective*. With the rise of insurance 'gaming becomes a symbol of the world', but only in a limited sense. Insurance is not a mere gamble. Gaming is an effective analogy for individual decisions based on probability analysis, which may or may not work out well. With insurance, by contrast, we are mostly confident that

---

[22] Despite his use of the present tense, it is important that Ewald was speaking historically.

things *will* work out well, and this confidence derives from aggregation. Whereas the decision-making model proposes that risk assessment gives us freedom (to decide), Ewald argues that it is insurance which contributes more decisively to freedom, because it releases us from fear. A positive risk assessment may suggest that acting is worthwhile, but if the stakes are high then the opportunity may be out of reach. Only if we find a way of distributing or managing exposure to that risk do we have the freedom to pursue it. Furthermore, Ewald argues that although insurance is 'collective' and creates 'mutualities', these also leave the actor relatively untouched. In this sense, the mutualities of insurance are different from earlier mutualities (such as family, religion, or trade union) which made more claims upon the individual.

The rise of insurance, then, made possible certain solutions to common problems. But according to Ewald, it also constituted certain challenges to existing liberal and (importantly) juridical ways of approaching these problems. In particular, challenges surround the issues of accidents and of distributions. These challenges are said to stem from risk in the collective, insurance sense, and are relevant to the questions considered in chapters 3 and 4.

Accidents and Distributions

So far as accidents are concerned, Ewald maintains that the 'technology' of risk considers risks across a population as a whole. Previously, an 'accident' was perceived at law as a unique and exceptional event between an author and a victim. The focus on *risks* challenges this by emphasising both statistical regularity, and expectation of occurrence. While discovery of regularity in human affairs does not in itself negate free will, it naturally leads us to seek solutions which do not emphasise the will of the actor so much. The focus on risks also tends to emphasise interdependence. Any action may create a risk. The action which does damage is nothing exceptional, and 'ill will' need not be involved: accidents are 'normalised'. Causation, previously vital, need not be emphasised at all. Insurance acts to pool the risks of all potential victims (who may also be potential authors of misfortune), and thus creates mutualities.

It is true that predictability and regularity in accident rates have made it harder to justify a focus on the defendant's state of mind in accident law. Indeed the 'fault' principle is generally not now defended in terms of state of mind at all, and it is partly for this reason that 'outcome responsibility', or other ways of justifying responsibility for outcomes, have become such a preoccupation of tort theorists in recent years. It is also true that the practice of insurance, including compulsory insurance cover in many crucial cases, challenges the monopoly of law in respect of accidents and threatens the juridical image of the event by overlapping with the law of tort. Insurance 'technology' underlies the whole practice of tort law. Without it, accident law would be relatively insignificant, because damages would be paid on few occasions.[23]

So far as distributions are concerned, Ewald argues that liberal thought regarded the natural attribution of goods and ills as just in itself. On this view, he claims that it was only deviations from the natural state of affairs that required correction, in order to vindicate the pre-existing order. For Ewald, the development of insurance directs attention away from a philosophy based upon 'natural order' and allows for societal definitions of what is just. It also establishes the justice of 'the proportional share'. He appears to argue that the 'philosophy of risk' is inherently interested in distributions (in the sense of fair shares), while liberal thought was more engaged with correcting deviations from the status quo. In Anglo-American legal theory, 'correcting deviations' would now most likely be captured through the Aristotelian terminology of 'corrective justice'.

Leaving aside Ewald's historical portrait of liberal thought, it is clear that modern liberals including many legal theorists have begun to pay close attention to distributive justice and have even borrowed 'insurance' ideas to some extent.[24] It should also be

---

[23] 'Insurance' here should be understood as including 'self-insurance'–management of exposure to liabilities within larger corporations.

[24] See the discussion of Coleman in ch 3 below, and Dworkin in ch 5 below.

said that corrective justice theorists with an interest in risk have been particularly inclined to see a continuity between corrective and distributive issues.[25] Nevertheless, the continuity is achieved partly by applying principles of personal responsibility to the questions of distributive as well as corrective justice. Although such theories frequently use ideas of risk, it is generally the decision-making and rational aspects of risk, rather than the statistical regularities, which they emphasise. On the whole, they are not theories of 'proportional share'.

There is another aspect of insurance emphasised by Ewald as part of the 'epistemological transformation' made possible by risk. The mutuality of those in the common risk pool (which is to say, their common exposure to risk) has been mentioned above. But Ewald also describes insurance as giving rise to 'solidarity'. In his analysis, solidarity and security are to some extent techniques used by the state to guarantee its own existence and assure itself of support. Use of solidarity underlines the role of insurance as a 'political technology'. Nevertheless, solidarity appears to be constituted mainly by insurance itself, which builds a close solidarity of *interests*, rather than through political will as such. Thus solidarity *enables* a social contract to be reached. This is part and parcel of Ewald's emphasis on 'technology' and know-how, above political factors. There is some further exploration of this, and comparison with egalitarian liberal approaches which might be thought to have 'solidaristic' overtones, in chapter 5 below.

It was noted above that Ewald's account of insurance and the provident state is historical, providing an important supplement to the histories of decision-making explored above, and at the same time posing certain important challenges to law. However, the provident state is threatened by some of the same developments in understanding of risk which were touched upon at the end of the last section. In particular, regularities are in question, not through lack of know-how, but if anything through growth of information and greater awareness among the general

---

[25] Examples in ch 4 below include Honoré, Coleman, and Ripstein.

population of risk management techniques. The definition of people in terms of risk factors does not always operate to their benefit, and the protection offered by mutuality may be contingent. If it becomes too easy to distinguish between good and bad risks, the principle of mutuality, that each risk should pay its fair price, will not provide security for all. Whether such developments also threaten solidarity depends on what solidarity is, and where it springs from. If it is merely an 'effect' of insurance technology, arising out of mutuality, then a perception that exposure is not so common is indeed threatening to solidarity. But if it develops as an independent political principle, then it may be *insurance* in its mutuality form which has only a contingent relationship with that principle. A given society may simply decide to extend cover beyond the existing risk pools of mutuality insurance. In chapter 5, these concepts will be tried out in respect of the threatened exclusion of individuals, for probabilistic reasons, from shared security.

3. Risk, Control, and Governmentality

Like François Ewald (above), the next set of perspectives is influenced by the ideas of Michel Foucault. These approaches are often grouped together and referred to as Foucauldian or 'governmentality' theories of risk, but to separate them allows us not only to highlight some of the distinctive ideas offered by Ewald, but also to note the more diverse and ambiguous implications of risk concepts both in criminology and in the broader study of 'governmentality'. In particular, Ewald stresses the use of risk technologies in providing significant elements of *security*, and also in building a 'philosophy of risk' which includes ideas of proportionate justice. His approach is concerned with *social* actuarialism.[26] While the engagement of criminologists could on

[26] Most of the original literature on actuarialism treated that idea as inherently collective and social, and would see no need to attach the epithet 'social'. This reflects the specific way in which ideas of regulatory power (below) were discussed by Foucault, and is taken here to be the core use of 'actuarialism'. More recently though, some writers have associated risk not with aggregation

one view be traced back to Simon's analysis of 'risk society',[27] which shares Ewald's emphasis on both aggregation and security, criminological theory has subsequently developed to consider some much more varied uses of risk as a technique of social control.

Simon's early article described how an emerging 'risk society' *Simon* governs and controls not through use of direct coercion nor by attempting to change behaviour, but through aggregating mechanisms and the 'channelling' of risks. Interestingly, Simon's article was more concerned with tort law and the handling of accidents than it was with criminal justice and penal policy. The ideas developed by Simon were later applied directly to penal policy through the articles of Feeley and Simon.[28] It is also important to note that the risk society outlined in Simon's article is not the same as the subject of Beck's rather better known *Risk Society* (which appeared in 1986 but was not translated into English until 1992). As explained below, Beck's risk society *optimistic* emerges only when there is 'reflexive' challenge to the actuarial and risk-based methods of control. Simon's risk society appears *pessimistic* in some respects to concern the gradual perfection and generalisation of such control.

The new techniques of control described by Feeley and Simon in subsequent articles by-pass individuals, dealing instead with populations or with changing the 'conditions' either of accidents or of crime. They do not depend on blame, and in the

and socialisation, but with the return of individualism in a very different guise. Thus, there has been recent discussion of 'privatized' actuarialism, in addition to the original version (see n 39 below).

[27] J Simon, 'The Emergence of a Risk Society: Insurance, Law and the State' (1987) 95 *Socialist Law Review* 61. Of course there have also been other influences—for example N Reichman, 'Managing Crime Risks: Toward an Insurance Based Model of Social Control' (1986) 8 *Research in Law, Deviance and Social Control* 252; S Cohen, *Visions of Social Control: Crime, Punishment and Classification* (Cambridge, Polity Press, 1985).

[28] See in particular M Feeley and J Simon 'The New Penology: Notes on the Emerging Strategy of Corrections and its Implications' (1992) 30 *Criminology* 449; M Feeley and J Simon, 'Actuarial Justice: The Emerging New Criminal Law' in D Nelken (ed), *The Futures of Criminology* (London, Sage, 1994).

sphere of criminal policy they are equally concerned with removing the *opportunity* for criminal acts.[29] This builds on Foucault's distinction between 'the disciplines' (including imprisonment), which worked on the body and were concerned with individuals' deviation from the norm; and 'regulatory' controls.[30] 'The disciplines' were the subject of Foucault's work on imprisonment, and were referred to by the term 'anatomo-politics'. 'Regulatory' controls were concerned with managing populations at an aggregate level. Foucault described these in terms of 'bio-politics'.

Commentators have generally treated the impact of social actuarialism as ambiguous. Most concede that aggregation, management and insurance bring clear benefits. However, there have also been concerns surrounding, in particular, the role of individuals as the subjects of regulatory power. Simon's early article expressly identifies a potential opposition between 'risk' defined in terms of regulatory techniques of aggregation and security, and what he calls 'sovereignty'. Sovereignty in his terms has something in common with the moral sovereignty of the individual to be found in liberalism, in the sense that he refers to 'self-understanding of the subject'—a very internal and personal vantage point. I have already explained above that liberalism is in some respects quite friendly to risk terminology (so long as it is not too statistical in form), regarding decision-making techniques as providing a natural way in which free and rational individuals might reach decisions. Thus many liberal approaches see no necessary distinction between what might be called individual sovereignty, and risk techniques; but there is a potential conflict over *collective* technology, as described by both

[29] Although this may involve a trend toward 'incapacitation' of certain groups, it may equally focus on victim behaviour and take the form of 'situational crime prevention'.

[30] M Foucault, *History of Sexuality* (London, Allen and Lane, 1979) vol I, cited for example by P O'Malley, 'Risk, Power and Crime Prevention' (1992) 21 *Economy and Society* 252. For more general discussion of the role of regulatory power, and of the origins of 'governmentality' in Foucault's writings, see M Dean, *Governmentality* (London, Sage, 1999).

Ewald and Simon, in distinction to individual reason. Importantly, as a gloss on Ewald's implication that the 'mutualities' created by insurance largely leave individuals free to conduct their lives as they will,[31] Simon suggests that both sovereignty and various forms of community are increasingly being annulled by the logic of insurance and risk, and especially their abstraction from personal responsibility. This raises issues which resurface in the discussion of insurance and responsibility in accident law (chapters 3 and 4 below).

There are potential objections to Simon's thesis. In particular, he argues that law (as the method by which harms are distributed in society) has been at the forefront of actuarialism and aggregation. This is repeated in the later arguments of Feeley and Simon, and of Ericson and Haggerty,[32] all of whom suggest that accident law in particular was in the vanguard of actuarialism, and is now completely absorbed by actuarial justice. There will be time to consider the connection or opposition between tort theory and actuarialism in chapter 3, where it will be suggested that we must be very careful in our interpretation of risk-based thinking in tort law. In particular, the language of risk is used quite extensively within law and economics, and some of the developments identified as establishing 'actuarialism' in tort law are equally steps on the way to an economic interpretation of tort liability. The law and economics movement has generally taken a form which, despite its utilitarianism and concentration on 'welfare', can be strongly contrasted with the precepts of social actuarialism as found in Simon's thesis.[33] In other words,

[31] Simon's starting point here is actually similar to Ewald's: he suggests that being relieved of the financial effects of one's actions operates to significantly enhance one's freedom.

[32] RV Ericson and KD Haggerty, *Policing the Risk Society* (Oxford, Clarendon Press, 1997).

[33] Feeley and Simon comment, in 'Actuarial Justice: The Emerging New Criminal Law', n 28 above, that law and economics, as a general school of legal thought, is importantly different from the actuarialism they discuss, in particular because of the preoccupation of law and economics with the individual response of rational actors. A similar point is developed in ch 3 below. However, they also suggest that the newest approaches to tort law are preoccupied with

commentators may be too quick to equate any interest in 'risk' and 'control' with social actuarialism.

There are continuing doubts too about how much evidence exists for the reported rise of 'actuarial justice' in criminal justice. 'Actuarial justice' is a quite specific term, which should not be applied without question to any and all attempts to prevent crime rather than to punish it. For Feeley and Simon, it is particularly exemplified by attempts to 'manipulate the public as a demographic mass or aggregate',[34] bypassing the minds of individuals altogether. In this terminology, there is a very sharp distinction between decision-making theories of risk on the one hand, which seek ways to empower individuals and perhaps even the group so far as decision-making is concerned, and actuarial justice on the other. According to Feeley and Simon, actuarial approaches (particularly incapacitation) treat individual actors as essentially 'inert' where decision-making is concerned, and do not depend on incentives but on manipulation of situations and minimisation of risk,[35] including management-through-custody of dangerous segments of the population. Comparing Simon's views with those of Ewald, one of the key issues is whether the techniques of risk, which are in both cases associated with social actuarialism and the collective, are liable to create new forms of solidarity and mutuality (Ewald's line), or to dehumanise and destroy non-instrumental forms of community (broadly the approach taken by Simon).

CASTEL   The Foucauldian analysis of a move from 'the disciplines' to 'bio-politics' has been applied in many other contexts, beyond the areas of accident law and penal policy concentrated upon here. For example, Castel suggests that in social work and other caring professions, there has been a shift from ideas of 'danger-

how to 'manage' accidents, and that they are therefore 'actuarial'. They do not comment on the rise of law and economics as an aspect of tort theory, nor could they predict that more recent arguments about tort and insurance would drift towards recommendation of a market insurance, rather than social insurance, solution.

[34] Op cit, n 33 above, p 175.
[35] *Ibid*, p 189.

ousness' to ideas of 'risk'.[36] Analysis of 'dangerousness' would centre on the characteristics of an individual who has in some way (perhaps through some confrontation) become defined as a threat. Dangerousness does to some extent depend on an analysis of probabilities, but it is an analysis which is performed on the basis of information concerning the *particular* individual. New forms of regulation described by Castel no longer depend upon surveillance in the same physical sense, switching instead to surveillance in the sense of 'systematic predetection' which is (incidentally) universal. No social class avoids surveillance. The disciplines depended upon a certain form of individualization, according to Castel, whereas the new forms of surveillance have no relation of immediacy with a subject. Indeed, he goes further, to argue that there *is* no subject. The new predictive policies primarily concern not individuals, but 'factors'. They aim to anticipate danger.

This can be linked with Simon's thesis that whether in terms of access to credit or in terms of the design of road systems, the new forms of regulation (based on actuarialism) aim to channel risk and avoid conflict. O'Malley memorably illustrates this by explaining that whereas the symbol of the disciplines was the panopticon, the symbol of the risk society (in its actuarial sense) would be the speed hump.[37] Castel suggests that the policies of prevention aim at 'a vast hygienist utopia', where calculative reason is applied by 'administrators of happiness for a life to which nothing ever happens'.[38] In rhetorical terms at least, nothing could be less like the liberal notion of responsible, active individuals pursuing the good life, which is so closely tied also to liberal treatments of 'risk'. But Castel's imagery is equally far removed both from Beck's idea of an individualised society in which each individual must take responsibility for planning their

[36] R Castel, 'From Dangerousness to Risk' in G Burchell *et al*, *The Foucault Effect*, n 21 above, p 281.

[37] P O'Malley (ed), *Crime and the Risk Society* (Aldershot, Dartmouth, 1998) xii.

[38] Castel, n 36 above, p 289.

own biography (below), and from Giddens' eulogising about the 'energising' properties of risk (the 'third way' approach).

As mentioned above, there have been further developments in the criminology of risk in recent years. One direction that this has taken is the identification of 'privatized actuarialism' alongside, and increasingly perhaps in the ascendant over, the social forms of actuarialism treated as central by Simon.[39] As O'Malley has suggested, the resurgence in language of 'responsibility' to be found in penal policy but also much more widely should not too quickly be dismissed as a merely temporary political development.[40] Nor should it be regarded as wholly separable from the idea of risk or even of actuarialism. Instead, O'Malley suggests that the role of risk in 'governmentality' is much more varied and suggestive of far greater political variations than has generally been noted within the literature which is derived from Foucault's analysis. Thus, even if we retain a sense that 'risk' should be analysed above all as a technique of governance, O'Malley emphasises that this technique need not contain the same type of political and philosophical implications outlined by Ewald and Simon in rather different ways. It is increasingly understood that 'governmentality' involves not only the development of aggregating techniques in pursuit of security and the general welfare, but also techniques of disaggregation and delegation of government functions to the private sphere.

A second example of evolution in the 'actuarial' interpretation of criminal justice is the attempt by Ericson and Haggerty to integrate the 'actuarial justice' thesis of Feeley and Simon, with the rather different 'risk society' thesis of Ulrich Beck.[41] For Ericson and Haggerty, the emphasis is on fragmentation in power and control, with the institutions of risk society (notably insurers) being motivated by an actuarial logic which always

---

[39] The expression 'privatized actuarialism' is used by P O'Malley, 'Risk and Responsibility' in A Barry, T Osborne and N Rose (eds), *Foucault and Political Reason* (London, UCL Press, 1996; London, Routledge, 2001).

[40] O'Malley, 'Risk, Power and Crime Prevention', n 30 above.

[41] RV Ericson and KD Haggerty, *Policing the Risk Society* (Oxford, Clarendon Press, 1997).

seeks the production of further information and leads to the generation of knowledge. The police and other agents of criminal justice are, according to Ericson and Haggerty, increasingly employed in supplying the information and reassurance required by actuarial institutions, to the detriment of their more traditional functions.

Importantly, the concerns raised by Ericson and Haggerty are very different from the possible disappearance of sovereignty which was of such concern to Simon. In particular, Ericson and Haggerty suggest that 'fragmentation signals inequality' in risk society; and that the apparatus of risk-management in respect of crime fosters the development not of freedom to lead one's life with security, but of 'foreboding and fear', thus encouraging people to withdraw into privatized lifestyles.[42] They also propose, like O'Malley, that this is not an alternative to the thesis of 'bio-power', but a continuation of it with a different strategic and political direction. Thus, they propose that the 'perfection of bio-power is self-governance'.[43] It has often been noted before that bio-power gains its effectiveness partly from the way that it fosters acquiescence or consensus among the regulated population,[44] but this goes further. The delegation of responsibility for risk management to individual decision-makers is in itself a technique of governance.

Ericson and Haggerty come a little closer to Beck's thesis, in particular by doubting the 'smooth cool surface' that Simon initially described as the hallmark of a risk (or actuarial) society[45]; and by emphasizing self-governance and the impact of obligations to manage risks upon individuals. They draw on Beck in suggesting that traditional political institutions are 'less and less the innovators in risk management, but merely agents . . . within

[42] *Ibid*, pp 451 and 450 respectively.

[43] *Ibid*, p 452.

[44] See for example, N Reichman, 'Managing Crime Risks', n 27 above, p 168. Reichman expresses concern that the appearance of consensus may numb our ability to recognise that power is deployed through insurance.

[45] Simon, n 27 above, p 79.

the technical systems of nonstate institutions'.[46] Differences remain, however. In particular, it will be explained below that Beck emphasises the *'reflexiveness'* of risk society, which is to say that it leads inherently to self-confrontation and questioning. These are in turn *politicising* effects. This aspect is missing both from the account of the rise of actuarial justice as a method of social control by the state; and from the much more decentralised risk activities described by Ericson and Haggerty.

Dispute about the political or technical nature of risk techniques is important for the study of risk and legal theory. For example, Simon illustrates the conflict between 'risk' and 'sovereignty' with reference to disagreement and protest concerning nuclear power. For Simon, the language of 'cost-benefit' employed in making siting decisions is not intelligible to citizen protestors who are later hauled from the site. Their stand is taken on moral and political grounds which he says are foreign to the 'cost-benefit discourse' of environmental impact studies.[47] Yet the popularity of Beck's *Risk Society* derives I would suggest partly and precisely from the way that it shows how the language of cost-benefit and of risk is capable of being critically understood by citizens and in this sense politicised in the emerging risk society. Some commentators, and particularly those retaining a social actuarial model, have presented 'risk' almost entirely in terms of institutional technique, and the perfection of control. Simon describes the governance of risk society in terms of the 'hum of integrated circuits', for example, and O'Malley emphasises that governmentality theory has often assumed that risk is a preferred technique of governance *because of* its connection with enhanced efficiency.[48] Ericson and Haggerty are preoccupied with the impact of institutionalised risk techniques. Both Beck, and some of the theorists of decision-making touched upon in 1 above, share an interest in the way that risks have *defied* control. Indeed, both see some hope in this very defiance.

---

[46] Ericson and Haggerty, n 41 above, p 119.

[47] Simon, n 27 above.

[48] O'Malley, 'Risk and Responsibility', n 39 above.

4. Risks and Hazards

The approaches considered above have been linked in many respects, despite their differences. It is possible to see their common origins in a more or less technical concept of risk, linked to decision-making, distribution or control in one way or another. In all of these approaches, risk is linked more to human techniques than to actual hazards. But increasingly, there are also very influential approaches where risks are closely related to hazards. In particular, I have so far said only a little about one of the most influential of all social theories with emphasis on risk, Ulrich Beck's *Risk Society*.

Beck argues that modernity is entering a 'reflexive' stage, in which there is growing awareness that industrialization has given rise to new risks, that these risks were not intended, and that despite the prevalence of 'risk techniques' they are not truly controllable or reliably measurable after all. Unlike the Foucauldian theorists, Beck urges that potential for political change stems from critical reflection (or, in his more precise terminology, 'self-confrontation') within modernity. Beck emphasises the existence of new types of risks *in the sense of hazards* within late modern societies. In particular, new hazards are not 'natural', but man-made. Beck describes these in terms of 'modernisation effects'; while Giddens refers similarly to 'manufactured risk'.[49] The link between risks and hazards is highlighted by comparing the role of 'risk' in 'risk society', with the role of wealth in class society. For Beck, class societies are dominated by scarcity and the distribution of wealth ('goods'); risk society is dominated by safety and the distribution of risks ('bads').

For both Beck and Giddens, newer risks are much less amenable to control than previous risks, especially through insurance, since many of them threaten one-off or catastrophic results. They are non-reciprocal, in the sense that some groups

[49] See for example, A Giddens, 'Risk and Responsibility', (1999) 62 *Modern Law Review* 1–10, at p 4: 'manufactured risk is risk created by the very progression of human development, especially by the progression of science and technology'.

and organisations disproportionately create them while others disproportionately suffer them; they are often global or at least international in their reach; and they are highly dependent on value judgment for their characterisation. There is not even agreement on whether the risks exist, and there is controversy over scientific and statistical evidence. Because of these risks, everyone recognises the sceptical nature of science, which until recently has been a well-kept secret.

It is important that in 'Risk Society', modernization has both positive and negative features. There is an increasing level of wealth, and security is greatly enhanced by techniques of risk control and insurance. However, certain risks are increasingly perceived as impervious to control. A sense of insecurity is rife despite all the relevant controls. The creation, distribution, and prevention of risks, rather than the creation and distribution of wealth, become the main preoccupations of risk society.

Both Beck and Giddens emphasise that one of the important features of risk in the new setting of 'risk societies' or reflexive modernity is simply that people link bad outcomes with decision-making. If something goes wrong, they tend to find a human cause, however far away in distance or time. In one sense this is simply an historical development of the logic outlined in both 1 and 2 above. It is true that risk in Beck's approach is linked with *hazard* at least as much as technique, because control no longer seems so complete, and safety and security are no longer guaranteed. The 'technology' of risk therefore breaks down. However, risk is not linked with 'fate', which was the concept from which risk was described as making a clean break in 1 above. On the contrary, almost all events in risk society can be seen as in some sense the result of human action. They may be unexpected events, but this does not alter the fact that they are the effect of human decisions. They are *side effects*. Though they are the product of decisions, they are not 'chosen'. The future can be much less clearly planned than we thought. Risk methods are implicated in these side effects chiefly because these methods minimise the appearance of hazards and make it appear that we can control the future.

48

Risk society is marked by awareness of the complexities of our actions' impact upon the world. The tendency to blame someone is an aspect of reflexive societies, but it is also important that in the circumstances of risk society, there is greater awareness of the difficulties of establishing cause (in a backward-looking sense), and of establishing what risks need to be considered for the future. The question of responsibility within risk society is generally considered important, but there is little to suggest how it should be resolved. Beck describes risk society as giving rise to a sense of 'organized *ir*responsibility' (emphasis added): no one is held to account. There are aspects of legal theory which overlap very directly with these sorts of concerns, and which arise in chapters 3 and 4. But in chapter 6, it is also explained that some recent approaches seek to build responsibility through a more inclusive approach to decision-making, which is also open about the limits of our knowledge.

It remains to comment more directly on the associations between the decision-making ideas in 1, and the risk society approach outlined here. It is tempting to assume that there must be a direct conflict between these approaches—that if we accept the portrayal of new-style risks and failures of control in risk society, then we must reject the decision-making model as outdated. This, I would suggest, is not the case. Indeed Bernstein's book illustrates very clearly how resilient and adaptable decision-making models have been to far-reaching changes in the nature of financial and natural risks. Changes in theories of decision-making under uncertainty even provide evidence for the kinds of changes referred to by Beck and Giddens. Volatility, uncertainty, interdependence: all of these factors are recognised by contemporary theorists of finance and markets. Nor should the 'financial context' be treated as 'esoteric' and in some way marginal.[50] Volatility and risk in financial markets have far-reaching implications for all aspects of life in contemporary societies,

[50] Lupton, n 1 above, p 8. Lupton implies that the idea of 'good risks' survives only in this esoteric context. My analysis of legal theory in Part II will suggest that the idea of a good risk, or at least of a risk worth taking, remains essential to some of legal theory's ideas of responsibility.

including (for example) pensions and welfare provision. To ignore this is perhaps to dwell too exclusively on a limited range of personal risks such as disease and toxicity.

5. Conclusion: Legal Theory and Perspectives on Risk

In what follows, I will suggest that the decision-making ideas explored as the first perspective here provide important elements of legal theory's intellectual heritage. Legal theory, however, has used such ideas in a distinctive and selective way, and in doing so it makes a particular contribution. Since this aspect of legal theory has rarely been explicit, it is not surprising that there are also some confusions and contradictions to confront.

The idea of risk as a collective technology, which was explored under heading 2, can also be identified as an important influence over legal theory, giving rise to rather different directions in the literature. Attention to this perspective helps us to explore some inner tensions in legal theory. These can be seen not only in the continuing debate over the role and functions of aspects of law, such as tort law in particular, but also in more abstract debates concerning the nature and role of distributive justice. The collective dimension has not been lacking from liberal legal theory here, but it has certainly had an ambiguous role.

Within the third perspective outlined above there is a rich array of literature concerning the use of risk as a technique of governance. On one dimension, this literature has a direct and instrumental impact on the styles of law-making and governance which may be adopted. But for our purposes, it is more significant that the theoretical developments touched on under this heading lead us to question the apparently rational, dispassionate nature of the collective and aggregating approach to risk. Recent doubts which affect these collective and aggregating approaches have seemed to lead towards greater individualisation, and it is tempting to conclude that this strengthens the claims of liberal theorists because it focuses back upon the individual. But as is explored in chapter 5 below, the kind of individualisation which has sometimes been observed in this context is not the same as the philosophical individualism of liberal legal theory. This is one reason why proponents of personal responsibility should be wary.

Finally, I outlined some elements of Beck's *Risk Society* which are of particular resonance for legal theory. In particular, Beck not only reinforces the sceptical elements of the governance theories, but also directs our attention to the changing role of individuals. According to Beck, individuals are increasingly required to be adept at decision-making in respect of risk, but they also become sceptical and critical of risk method. Despite a passing resemblance, these individuals have a very different role from the planning, preferring, and reasoning individuals of liberalism. Beck's insights therefore add some critical notes to our central themes of agency and responsibility. But his writings also turn our attention to the particular questions of environmental decision-making, precaution, and uncertainty, where this book finally arrives.

Part II. Risks in Legal Theory—Some Core Instances

3
Risks, Accidents and Insurance

1. Introduction to Chapters 3 and 4

The actuarial and insurance-based approaches to risk explored in chapter 2 (parts (b) and (c)) did not differentiate between risks on the basis of who or what caused them, unless this was necessary for some reason—for example, to protect principles of mutuality. Risk techniques were involved with classifying exposure to possible loss, and resolving possible sources of insecurity. Risks were thought about in an essentially prospective way, in terms of a calculable exposure to hazard across a group, and insecurity was avoided using a variety of techniques. These included minimization, loss-spreading, and risk channelling. Ewald contrasted this aggregating approach with the pre-existing 'juridical' notion, which had it that accidents were the product of individual will and allegedly made liability depend on 'ill will'. For Ewald, this had little to do with risk, which he perceived as an inherently collective term.

I have already suggested however that concentration on 'individual will' could itself be closely associated with 'risk', if risk is perceived in a decision-making sense with a focus on individuals and especially upon the vindication of agency. Instead of statistical regularity and predictability, this approach would emphasise agency and choice. It would not necessarily emphasise culpability. Thus the connections between theories of tort law, and risk, have never been simple and have settled around a major fault-line that can be referred back to different perspectives on risk.

In the next two chapters, I concentrate on two very different strands in understanding aspects of tort law and (to a lesser extent) contract law as they relate to accidental damage, and in each case I explore some of the ways that risk is treated as central. In both instances, many theorists use the vocabulary of risk. Yet the theories are not often read or discussed in such a way that the importance of this is noted. There is little overt discussion of what is meant by the word 'risk', and of the technical solutions and devices of argument that may be implied by its use. Thus they illustrate that risk is sometimes seized upon within legal theory as an explanatory device, without necessarily being subjected to close attention in its own right.[1]

As already hinted, we can (loosely) associate these two strands in tort theory with different aspects of thinking about risk. To be specific, they may be connected with the actuarial/collective,[2] and the agent-focused, respectively. But we will have to be aware that such associations are only tentative and preliminary. Furthermore, it will be part of the argument in the next two chapters that attempts to keep the two strands apart do not always succeed.

The first set of responses tends to treat 'accidents' (or accidental harm) as a social problem to be dealt with in the most effective way. This is not to say that such approaches are necessarily empty of ideas about fairness or responsibility. However, they can be said to be 'collective' in the sense that the problem of accidents is seen as potentially relevant to the population as a whole. Importantly, they look prospectively at the likelihood of damage, not retrospectively at events and participants. Thus they tend to abstract from individual instances to look at problems in the round. Not surprisingly, they tend to treat civil

---

[1] Admittedly there have been some technical discussions of risk and probability. Authors seek to incorporate 'a' risk perspective based on such expertise, in order to illuminate the answers to particular questions. The point here is that there is little discussion of the heritage and philosophical implications of using risk expertise; nor of the alternatives to probabilistic method.

[2] I am here referring to 'actuarialism' in its central, social form, as outlined in ch 2 above. However, the proposed shift to first party insurance in accident law itself raises the issue of fundamental change in the nature of insurance-based solutions, and this is discussed further in this chapter.

liability as part of a continuum with insurance, so we must decide whether they display the features of 'actuarial' approaches described in the chapter above.

Something else also begins to emerge through this concentration on the legal theoretical literature relating to accident law and insurance, and the controversies which have become increasingly familiar there. In chapter 2, it has been explained that 'insurance' was credited with significant influence in the evolution of regulatory techniques of governance. Subject to some of the later contributions to the literature on 'governmentality', there has been an emphasis predominantly on the emergence of insurance as a technique or technology, and it has been said that social and philosophical implications are largely considered as flowing from this. Within legal theory, we find that insurance is not regarded as a single technique, and furthermore that its technical innovations are not accorded primary importance. They are even underplayed. Instead, where insurance is noted as being important at all, there is considerable concern with distributive and allocative fairness, as well as with effectiveness, and this tends to underline that both the type and the nature of insurance are crucial to many questions. Also, considerable attention is now given to what type of political philosophy underlies insurance solutions. In a sense this challenges one of Ewald's lines of argument, to the effect that the solutions to common problems adopted in very different jurisdictions could nevertheless be understood more clearly in light of a *common* idea of 'insurance', understood particularly in the light of common technical features.

This challenge begins to emerge in the present chapter with the arguments about distinction or continuity as between first and third party insurance in terms both of fairness and of practical impact. I suggest that the challenge is only partially successful, and in chapter 4 I suggest that the insurance mechanism itself should be taken more seriously by those theorists who seek to approach tort law in terms of responsibility, since its implications for responsibility are sometimes overlooked or not well understood. In chapter 5, the challenge to the rather

57

single or unitary idea of insurance focuses instead on possible distinctions between mutuality and solidarity-based insurance and on the contingent nature of solidarity. And in the same chapter, it is asked whether there is a shift in the nature and role of insurance such that insurance no longer emphasises aggregation with solidarity as an 'effect'; rather, it begins to emphasise differentiation, so that discrimination between classes and individuals becomes its major stock in trade.

The second set of responses to accident law, considered in chapter 4, tends to start 'close up' to individual participants, treating accidental harms as the effects of individual actions. This is the traditional core of tort theory, and recalls Ewald's sketch of the 'juridical' approach to accidents. Yet it is not necessarily identical to the portrait provided by Ewald. In recent years, a number of theorists have tried to explain, using notions of risk, why and when there is individual responsibility for the outcomes of one's actions sufficient to lead to liability. Indeed, theories employing risk as part of the solution to such questions are now so widespread that the discussion in chapter 4 must be highly selective.[3] Hurd has even argued that it is not possible to make sense of the idea of negligence in tort law without reference to risk.[4] For her, the choice is between the 'calculus of risk' approaches accepting the 'Hand formula' for breach of duty (which are consequentialist and exemplified by Priest's first principle, below), and (alternatively) 'deontological' attempts to use risk. The latter are all doomed to fail, in her view.[5]

[3] Particular focus is dedicated to the respective theories of Honoré and Ripstein. Other theorists of tort law who couch their discussion in terms of risk are Fletcher, Coleman, Perry, Schroeder, and Epstein, and there is room only for occasional reference to some of these.

[4] H Hurd, 'The Deontology of Negligence' (1996) 76 *Boston University Law Review* 249–72.

[5] In brief, Hurd considers that there cannot be a moral duty not to impose a risk. This is partly a matter of definition. Hurd proposes that risks and outcomes must be kept separate, because to take a risk is to take the chance of a bad outcome. The chance cannot itself be the outcome. Tort liability on the other hand attaches only to outcomes. The 'responsibility' theories explored in ch 4 respect Hurd's distinction between risks and outcomes, but do not adopt the 'calculus

Hurd's claim is of course controversial, but it indicates how familiar the vocabulary of risk has become in the context of tort theory. She is not alone in taking as read the centrality of risk.[6] I have suggested above that this familiarity is not met by any sufficient attempt to explore the concept or concepts of risk being employed in tort theory, nor to check them for completeness or coherence. If a 'background' body of work on risk is referred to, it is generally associated with probabilities and statistical know-how. I am therefore going to ask some questions about the nature and implications of the way that legal theory has employed 'risk' terminology in this context.

In chapter 4, then, it will be time to update the sketch of legal theory's approach to accidents. Legal theory has progressively distanced itself from the idea that 'culpability' holds the key to accident law. 'Responsibility' theories have progressively used more references to 'risk' in attempting to articulate the basis of liability, but this is a different idea from the prospective form of risk employed by Ewald.

Responsibility theories of tort law have largely approached 'risks' not as associated with classifications or observed regularities, but as derived from risk-taking behaviour. That is to say, a bad outcome will be traced back to human action or inaction on specific occasions. Use of 'risk' in this sense focuses on the influence of human agency on outcomes. In some variants of liberal theory, the idea of risk-taking is used to encapsulate the special relationship between individual agents and the outcomes

of risk' approach. They focus on outcomes while using risk as a step on the way to justifying responsibility. Thus they show that there are further possibilities outside Hurd's analysis. But further, there are also developments which make more respectable a blurring of chances and outcomes, and these are considered at the end of ch 4.

[6] Perry, for example says that risk 'is one of the central concepts in modern tort law', S Perry, 'Risk, Harm and Responsibility' in D Owen (ed), *Philosophical Foundations of Tort Law* (Oxford, Clarendon Press, 1995); and Porat and Stein consider that the 'modern' phase of tort law (not the most recent) has been concerned with wrongful exposure to risk, and materialisation of that risk. See: A Porat and A Stein, *Tort Law Under Uncertainty* (Oxford, OUP, 2001).

of their actions in the world, forming the basis of outcome responsibility. Although theorists who prefer a 'responsibility' approach have sometimes been critical of 'insurance' approaches to tort law for omitting issues of responsibility and, sometimes, of fairness, I will also suggest that the approaches based on outcome responsibility tend to get drawn into distributive issues, and even that they are fundamentally incomplete in their own terms without consideration of such issues.

But equally importantly, the concentration on outcome responsibility is only one aspect of the liberal approach to risks. Liberal theory does not always concern itself with the question of how the outcomes of actions are related to the actors in question. Rather, liberal theory sometimes constructs a hypothetical moment, and proposes what would, in that moment, be the preferred solution to the questions posed. The precise significance of insights gleaned this way can of course be debated, but the existence of a dichotomy between these two sorts of approach is easy to overlook, and the boundary between them is easily blurred. It will be suggested that Dworkin, for example, gives the rhetorical impression that he is dealing with responsibility for outcomes where one's own life is concerned, but his theory more truly concerns 'imagined decisions', and the idea that appropriate responses can be pinpointed in this way.

At the end of chapter 4, I pause to consider in outline a separate idea. It is sometimes mooted that the law has begun to provide compensation for risk per se—perhaps that exposure to risk has become so important both from the point of view of victims and from the point of view of defining wrongdoing that risk has become a recoverable kind of damage in itself. Some even claim that tort law must treat risk as damage if it is to avoid making arbitrary distinctions between morally equivalent risk-takers.

The weight of current opinion holds, in my view correctly, that this is a misconception which does not correctly interpret the existing case law. It is also incompatible with underlying theories of tort law whether these are expressed in terms of responsibility or of risk 'calculus'. Risk is not, so far, a form of recoverable damage. Indeed, 'risk' has arisen as a central term in this context mainly because of its connection with outcomes, rather than because of a concern with the wrongfulness of exposure to risk in an abstract sense. However, the developments in question are still rightly seen as being of interest, since they illustrate not only a move to embrace some statistical methods of proving causation, but also some major challenges in defining the current boundaries between risk and outcome.

2. Tort Law, Risk Control, and Insurance

As discussed in chapter 2, it was often claimed in the earlier literature surrounding risk and criminology that tort law was in the vanguard of developing 'actuarial justice'. It was even suggested that actuarialism had become *the* language of tort law.[7] It has already been pointed out here that there are a variety of sources for discussion of 'risk', and even of 'control' via risk, in tort law and tort theory, and that not all of these instances are necessarily to be identified with 'actuarialism'.[8] This can be illustrated through the history of attempts to argue that tort is best understood as carrying out an insurance function, or (alternatively) that tort would best be replaced by some sort of insurance mechanism. In one respect, this is of direct interest to the present enquiry because of the different forms of insurance which have, in recent years, been identified as the best potential replacements for tort law. But equally, attention to the intellectual path by which such conclusions has been reached can be compared and to some extent contrasted with the 'actuarialism' of, for example, Feeley and Simon, as well as Ewald.

One way of initiating this enquiry is through the account given by George Priest.[9] Priest described the emerging

---

[7] M Feeley and J Simon, 'Actuarial Justice: The Emerging New Criminal Law', in D Nelken (ed), *The Futures of Criminology* (London, Sage, 1994) discussed in ch 2 above.

[8] See ch 2 above, n 33.

[9] What follows draws chiefly on the most broadly-expressed of Priest's articles on the subject: G Priest, 'The New Legal Structure of Risk Control' (1990)

preoccupation of American tort law with risk in terms of the history of *an idea*. American courts, he said, had come to accept the 'internalisation of risk' as a general principle. This had led to the development of two principles. The first (relating to control) was more widely accepted than the second (relating to distribution). Certainly, the incentive-and-distribution system defined by Priest's principles appears to remain highly centralised and subject to rational planning, this time on the part of the courts under the guidance of economic theory of a particular type, and is in this sense compatible with the idea that risk is a mechanism of 'governance'. But we should be more explicit on the question of whether Priest's two principles are truly 'actuarial', while at the same time considering some philosophical issues stemming from the approach to accidents that they encapsulate.

It is true that both principles are *functional*, in that they aim at certain social goals; it is also true that Priest distinguishes these goals from an older, culpability-based approach. But I shall say below that the first principle in particular is not like actuarial justice. The second might be closer, but it is described by Priest as less broadly accepted; and he also argues that it is not properly pursued through tort law. Partly because of its two party, ex post form, and its interest in who did what and with what consequences, tort is just not actuarial enough to fulfil the distributive function. Thus, Priest has argued (in common with a number of others) that tort should be reformed, with an eye particularly on its 'true' insurance function.

Two Principles

1. Risk control function

The over all reason for suggesting that Priest's first principle, of risk control, is not truly actuarial is that it does not seek to avoid, channel, or otherwise deal with risk in a manner focused on

119 (4) *Daedalus* 207–27. This article is also referred to extensively by RV Ericson and KD Haggerty, *Policing the Risk Society* (Oxford, Clarendon, 1997) discussed in ch 2 above. See also (for example) G Priest, 'The Invention of Enterprise Liability: A Critical History of the Intellectual Foundations of Modern Tort Law' (1985) 14 *Legal Studies* 461–527.

populations and by-passing the individual will; nor does it accept damage and risks as the outcomes of impersonal 'states of affairs' or 'situations'. On the contrary, it is geared to the production of incentives to act directly on the will, and assumes that individual behaviour in the course of risky activities can be altered through carefully structured liability rules. Thus it is dependent on individual rationality and responsiveness to incentives, just as the 'old penology' described by Feeley and Simon relied on the idea of general deterrence. It further assumes that damage flows from individual action. It is simply an economic variation of the idea that individuals will act rationally in the face of incentives, and to neglect this is probably to assume rather too readily that discussion of 'risk' must *necessarily* involve abstraction from individual will.

On the other hand, what the first principle does have in common with 'actuarialism' is observation of the 'normalization' of risk-creation, which is also a familiar feature of the literature concerning crime in the risk society. The incentive system does, in a sense, replace an earlier 'culpability' notion, but not by removing the notion of responsibility, which Priest considers to be considerably enhanced by the principles he describes.[10]

Priest's first principle is familiar to most tort lawyers as a basic economic approach to negligence. It holds that tort law can and should create incentives to invest in safety, but only to a certain point. In particular, tort can create incentives to reduce the accident rate to an appropriate level, expressed in economic terms. Risks should be reduced so long as the cost of reducing them is lower than the expected benefits, in terms of liability avoided. This is captured by the 'Hand formula' for expressing negligence or breach of duty. There is negligence wherever the likelihood of injury combined with the likely cost of injury (generally though controversially equated with the likely cost of full compensation) is greater than the costs of precautions, since in

[10] 'To my mind, far from incorporating a diminished view of individual responsibility, the shift of the law's purpose toward risk control represents a vastly expanded commitment to personal responsibility', G Priest, 'The New Legal Structure of Risk Control', n 9 above, p 214.

all these cases (and not in others) precautions were cost-justified and should have been taken.

This approach clearly constitutes an application of 'expectancy value', discussed in chapter 1(a) above, with the economic costs of safety and of potential injury providing the key values. It will be clear that the judgment of liability cannot retrospectively make the exchange efficient since it will add extra costs into the mix; it can only provide incentives to invest. Therefore, it operates by seeking to guide future patterns of risk-taking.

For Priest, this is an expression not of an amoral approach, but of a moral approach which is specifically utilitarian. The first principle sets a standard for risk-taking. It provides the most widely-encountered economic interpretation of the fault principle and the objective standard of care in negligence. In other words, the principle could potentially be understood not only in terms of incentives, but also in terms of whether conduct was at fault. If approached in this way, its distinctive feature is that fault is understood only in terms of whether the amount spent on risk reduction was 'efficient'.

Of course there are many possible objections to such a standard. It is based on mathematical expectancy value, treating the imposition of risks toward others in exactly the same way as if the risks had been self-imposed. The standard thus does not 'respect the separateness of persons', because risk-creators are entitled to expose others to risks up to an 'efficient' level judged relative to the mathematical cost to the risk-creator of avoiding the risk. Interestingly, this same point can be amplified by applying ideas derived from the risk assessment paradigm. In physical injury cases particularly, the principle does not allow for proper consideration to be given to risk aversion. The possibility of a financial penalty taking the form of compensation is not likely to create the same aversion in the risk-creator as likelihood of physical harm would create in the potential victim. Thus the 'utility' of the sums to be used in the calculation is not considered, and this is a major flaw in the 'expectancy value' calculation applied if we are concerned with people's preferences.

Expectancy value will be *differently* judged from different perspectives. Yet the principle is discussed as a *general* principle of welfare economics. For this reason, the 'contractual alternatives', which appear to give more consideration to what would be chosen by people who are potential victims, may have a head start.

2. Distributive principle: best insurer

The second principle identified by Priest is the one that he regards as more controversial. Its acceptance, he says, has always been less uniform. And indeed the exact link between tort and insurance has remained highly controversial. Stapleton, for example, denies that either insurability, or actual insurance cover, have been major considerations for courts dealing with negligence cases.

Whereas the first principle is a mechanism for achieving appropriate levels of safety, the second is a principle of insurance. It proposes that where risks cannot or should not be prevented, their burden should be spread. Liability should therefore be attached to the party who is in the best position to insure, or otherwise to spread the risk (for example, by raising prices). One of the reasons why this is controversial is simply that it is not at all clear that courts actually reason in this way in very many cases.

But it should be noted that this principle also leads to the broader idea that insurance is either a direct function of tort law, or a direct alternative to tort law, or both. Acceptance of the second principle is not the only route to this broader conclusion that tort and insurance are directly related (whether as equivalents or alternatives). Another route to the same conclusion is the observation that *in effect*, people in general (including therefore those who are most likely to be victims of accidents) pay a premium towards the funding of future tort damages, whether through their own insurance policies, through general taxation funding aspects of the tort system, or through the prices of products that they buy. This alternative route does not depend at all on observation of what courts seek to do through the damages remedy. It turns on the actual *impact* of liability judgments.

Concentrating for the moment on the distributive principle in the precise form suggested by Priest, there is a problem of compatibility with the first principle. If liability judgments deter (principle 1), how can further liability judgments (those designed to prompt distribution of the risks in principle 2) fail to deter further? If they do deter further, then there will, in terms of the first principle, be over-deterrence. If on the other hand the possibility of spreading the risks through insurance avoids the problem of over-deterrence, so that risk-creators are no longer afraid of liability, then the same opportunity to spread the risks would also render ineffective the whole pattern of incentives provided by tort law through principle 1. Potential defendants would simply insure *instead of* spending on safety, and principle two would simply cancel out principle one. We could perhaps correct this by building in separate ideas, such as insurer pressure for investment in safety, but if we did this then the theory would be quite different, and the design of liability systems might require more than economic expertise. While we might coherently want to deal differently with unacceptable risks on the one hand (avoid them) and with the effects of acceptable risks on the other (pool them), it is very hard to see how both functions could be performed by one and the same remedy, through tort law. The second principle therefore raises the question of whether tort law has any deterrent effect, given the possibility of insurance.

But we should leave this potential conflict aside, and concentrate on principle 2 *per se*. It is in respect of this second principle that Priest's argument proposes the greatest retreat from individual responsibility, asserting that in such cases trials are no longer much concerned with the specific parties, but only with where losses of the relevant type will ultimately fall. Perhaps it is for exactly the same reason that Priest believes tort is most defective in respect of this second principle. In this principle, he suggests that courts regard the parties simply as 'representatives of generic categories of actors'. So, for example, manufacturers may be regarded as better able to spread the risks of injuries from products than are consumers, and local authorities more able to spread the risks of injuries from playground equipment than individual parents and children. The former parties therefore ought to be liable in order to provide incentives to insure, even if their products and playgrounds did not fall below a standard of safety and were in no sense excessively dangerous.

By thinking in terms of categories, this second principle has something in common with the actuarial approaches which was lacking from the efficiency principle, above. The second principle seeks an aggregating, risk-pooling effect. The first principle could be described without distortion as a principle of control, but at some level it appealed to individual responsiveness. Priest describes it in terms of a massive extension of responsibility, not a refutation of responsibility. We could add that it links responsibility with the opportunity to do something to minimise the risk (albeit only to an efficient level). The second principle bypasses the parties more completely. The 'best insurer' principle might not even require causation to be proved. The principle can be seen as being directed simply at providing security, whereas security was often not provided by principle 1, which offered compensation only in the event of *inefficient* risk-taking. Yet it is not a proper prudential principle. It proposes merely that allocation be performed in order to *gain access to* the benefits of risk technology—that is, to insurance. It is insurance, not tort, which distributes the loss. Priest expressly suggests that this solution has, in the US, to some extent been made necessary by the failings of other dimensions of social security. Courts are trying to plug the gaps in social insurance, through tort law. But his preferred solution is based in first party insurance.

The First Party Solution: Victim Responsibility?

It has been urged both by Priest and, in the UK, by Patrick Atiyah that first party insurance would be a much fairer and cheaper means of achieving the distributive goals which both believe are being sought (ineffectively) by tort law. For Priest, first party liability would also avoid the current insurance crisis suffered by important activities in the United States. He explains how liability law has led to withdrawal of insurance over a broad spectrum of activity, and thus not only to cancellation of new products but also to withdrawal of such services as playgrounds and high-risk aspects of medical care such as midwifery. Thus for Priest, the combination of a liability-focus in insurance methods, with excessive payments out in the case of liability, has led to a situation where tort strives to achieve an insurance goal, but does so defectively, and with considerable adverse effects.

Atiyah's analysis of the failures of tort as insurance is slightly different, yet in most respects compatible with Priest's.[11] Atiyah emphasises the question of whether tort law provides a form of insurance cover for accidental injuries which people would choose, if a salesperson were to offer it to them. His argument is that individuals would never opt for the cover provided by tort law at the price at which it is offered. The 'policy' contains too many exceptions and exclusions, including above all the fault principle however it is understood; it pays out only after years of legal argument and litigation; and because of the high compensation awards made in the relatively few successful cases, it is extremely expensive. Atiyah's point is that far from achieving an acceptable level of financial security at a reasonable price, as insurance is generally designed to do, tort leaves a great deal of insecurity and uncertainty, and confines its high payments to the few who can succeed in litigation. Thus its price is too high, and its attempt to deliver security is defective, if it is approached as a form of insurance. There is of course a counter-argument that tort should not be approached as a form of insurance at all. But as noted above, this has to deal with the argument that at present, we all pay for the tort system; and (more dubiously perhaps) that on the whole, we could assess in advance what the likely over all costs of injury will be. The argument is that tort operates *like* an insurance system, and it also depends upon insurance for liability awards to have any meaning. Proponents

[11] P Atiyah, 'Personal Injuries in the Twenty First Century: Thinking the Unthinkable' in P Birks (ed), *Wrongs and Remedies in the Twenty-First Century* (Oxford, OUP, 1996).

of the 'insurance' approach to tort law could also argue that to ignore the predictable nature of accidents is to close one's eyes quite wilfully to statistical observations about the world.

It certainly is arguable that the negotiation of conditions and the extent of cover should not be set without any input from those who are most likely both to pay the cost of premiums and to be exposed to the risks in question. But on the other hand, it is not at all clear that the first party insurance solution, or the contractual alternative which will be explored below, genuinely supposes that such negotiation would take place. That 'negotiation' remains hypothetical in both forms. In each case, the proponents consider (in reality) that they have established the rational level of insurance cover that would be decided upon by the 'purchaser' of insurance. This is one reason among others for suggesting that liberal theory is unlike the neo-liberal solutions in these cases, a comparison which is further pursued in chapter 5.

Atiyah also emphasises another argument for first party insurance. According to this argument, a new reliance on first party insurance would also underline the responsibility of individuals for managing their own security. When compared with his original work on accident law, this shows the mixed possibilities associated with insurance. As is well known, Atiyah moved from proposing a state-sponsored collective insurance scheme in the 1970s, to proposing commercial first party insurance for most or all risks in the 1990s.[12] The reason given for this is partly one of perceived practicability in light of an observed electoral preference for low tax policies over many years. But to back this up, he includes a direct appeal to responsibility for one's own security. At a minimum, this shows the truth of O'Malley's argument that 'actuarialism' may be associated with more than one sort of political perspective. But it is not at all clear how far Atiyah means to take the idea of personal responsibility. In chapter 5,

[12] PS Atiyah and P Cane, *Accidents, Compensation and the Law* (London, Butterworths, 1970); PS Atiyah, *The Damages Lottery*, (Oxford, Hart, 1997); ch 1 above.

some different variations of 'individual responsibility' for one's own security will be visited and discussed. On some interpretations, responsibility for first party insurance implies great reductions in personal security. Any proposed shift to first party insurance should be tested by attention to the likely effects of such a move.

Among various criticisms of the insurance approach to tort law, Stapleton's is particularly interesting because it begins by emphasising the multiple possibilities of insurance and the diversity in philosophy and attitude to responsibility which might underlie these.[13] Stapleton is right to argue that different approaches to insurance, stretching from social insurance to first party private insurance, are possible, and that the choice between these (or between these and a 'non-insurance' interpretation of tort law) is more than a purely practical matter. However, Stapleton is single-minded in her attempt to bury 'tort as insurance' and possibly does not always fairly represent the arguments of some of those, like Priest but also Coleman (below) who argue for limits to tort law at least in some contexts, on the basis that better contractual and insurance alternatives exist. I also suggest that a philosophically and politically preferred alternative needs to be examined by reference to its actual impact and whether, for example, it is counterproductive. Although the choice is, as Stapleton says, neither purely factual nor based on objectively agreeable grounds, to ignore the effects (rather than the objectives) of any given approach to insurance and liability is to take the chance of being 'blindly' ideological.

Stapleton contrasts the first party insurance approaches with arguments for the socialisation of risk. The latter she says has been a trend based essentially on the idea that where there are risks or hazards, their alleviation should be seen as a shared concern (we 'are all in it together'). Even so such ideas while they prioritise the need to provide compensation do not necessarily

[13] J Stapleton, 'Tort, Insurance and Ideology' (1995) 58 *Modern Law Review* 820–845; ch 1 above.

rule out a special responsibility on the part of harm-creators. For example, those who create risks may be required to pay more generously into appropriate funds. Insurance of this type may be part of the evolution of socialised and collective solutions, but attitudes to risk *creation* may still vary. First party insurance on the other hand places the cost of insuring with the potential victim, and Stapleton argues that this makes it essentially unfair. Thus she argues that while socialised risk allowed for different attitudes to responsibility and deterrence, to shift from third party insurance (purchased by risk-creators) to first party insurance (purchased by potential victims) is inherently to enrich risk-creators at the expense of those whom they may harm. Thus there is an argument about the distribution of the costs of insurance which is based on fairness between different groups.

Unfortunately, Stapleton does not turn her attention to one of the key elements in the argument for avoiding third party (liability) insurance. That is, that potential victims end up paying anyway for the tort system, and that they do not get good value for money. She retains a focus on who *initially* pays a premium, not on who *ultimately* bears the cost. Stapleton says that it is 'astonishing and counter-intuitive' to argue that potential plaintiffs should receive *less* protection from tort, in order to protect their interests. As it happens, 'risk theorists' of the statistical school have never been concerned about whether their proposals will appear 'counter-intuitive' to lawyers. They tend, indeed, to argue that intuitions can mislead and can reflect a habit of taking situations at their face value. Argument on the basis of statistical probabilities is designed at least in part to avoid this kind of susceptibility.[14] But in any case, the argument is less astonishing if recast in the terms in which it is actually offered: that potential *victims* should be required to spend less on costly provision against accidental damage, given that tort currently provides more such provision than is justified, subject to too many conditions, and at their expense.

---

[14] See for example R Sparks, 'Degrees of Estrangement' (2001) 5 *Theoretical Criminology* 159–76, commenting on the argument that use of statistical probabilities will improve decision-making in respect of reoffending.

In other words, it is intended that cheaper insurance should be provided in place of expensive tort, on the basis that the costs are ultimately the potential victim's in any event. Once again, the insurance theorists look prospectively at the risk and ask how it could best be dealt with. That this is a technique not unknown in some more hypothetical aspects of liberal theory is explored in chapter 5 below. But while Stapleton says that both tort and socialised risk exemplify hostility to a 'victim pays' morality, the 'tort as insurance' theorists are proposing that tort law is itself, in effect though not by design, a victim pays approach. They do not object to this, except in the sense that the price is too high.

In fact, this continuing debate involves untested assumptions on both sides. The 'insurance' theorists assume that in a shift to first party insurance, the costs to potential victims will not rise, and should fall; and that coverage (though not level of payments) would be improved rather than becoming patchier. This rests on a number of assumptions including the idea that the current policy-holders pass on the cost of insurance to their customers[15] (and that in a reciprocal insurance arrangement, the costs are shared); and also rests on many assumptions about the nature of the insurance industry and its ability and willingness to provide universal coverage. For her part, Stapleton assumes that the costs of insuring genuinely lie with the policy-holder, whoever that may be, and does not consider whether these costs are, in a third party insurance system, passed on to consumers and others through pricing.

There is perhaps a more fundamental difference of view between these different approaches to tort and insurance which goes deeper than the available evidence, and perhaps explains why there has been little attempt to seek further evidence. This is the question of whether accidents are primarily to be approached in terms of individual instances of human interac-

[15] We might question, for example, whether competition in the product market would prevent a negligent producer from shifting costs to consumers via prices, whether those costs were derived from increased premiums charged by insurers, or from the effect on profit margins where there is a form of 'self-insurance' at work.

tion, treating human agency as all-important and thus focusing on responsibility, blame, and incentive; or whether they should rather be approached as broadly predictable occurrences which can be statistically explored and therefore dealt with in advance through insurance. Here there is a persisting tension between statistical observation that all social arrangements create accidents, which then require to be dealt with, and the more individualistic idea that action gives rise to effects, which ought to be linked back through the idea of responsibility. While it is correct to say that different approaches to responsibility come into play through these arguments, this basic difference relates more directly to the very perception of what risk is about.

It seems very unlikely that proponents of the first party insurance solution, such as Atiyah, would be willing to follow through the full implications of a personal responsibility approach. Though some of Atiyah's comments seem to point to an 'own two feet' or 'asocial' philosophy,[16] it is by no means clear that such a philosophy really motivates the suggested move to first party insurance. It is equally possible that frustration with a tort system operating without full appreciation of its costs, and of the genuine connections between the interests of potential victims and of risk creators, has spurred theorists to look for solutions which will be more acceptable in today's supposed political climate than the original, social insurance version.

But we should be wary. Whatever the motivation for suggesting that first party insurance would be an improvement, the argument that people should be more aware of the trade-offs between security and the benefits of risk-taking should not be allowed to slip without further consideration into full scale victim responsibility. Opponents of this approach are right to

---

[16] PS Atiyah, *The Damages Lottery*, n 12 above, 140–43. Atiyah suggests there is a decline in 'blame' culture and greater acceptance that people must make more provision for themselves, rather than expecting governments to do it for them. It is Howarth who describes Atiyah's proposals for replacing tort law as amounting to an 'asocial individual responsibility regime'. See D Howarth, 'Three Forms of Responsibility: On the Relationship between Tort Law and the Welfare State' (2001) 60 *Cambridge Law Journal* 553–580, 565.

sense that there is potential for a major shift in practice, with considerable political and philosophical implications. At present, defenders of tort law provide little evidence of what would happen in such a shift, being more concerned with moral argument. But this should not lead us to accept the empirical assumptions of the 'first party insurance' proponents by default. The reasons for disagreement between the two factions should be seen as, in a sense, rather *more* than 'ideological'. While it is important to be clear about differences in philosophy, it is also important not to design legal systems on the basis of philosophy alone, without regard to effects.

So despite Atiyah's brief remarks about responsibility, it is possible that the attractions of insurance, to the proponents of first party solutions, remain the same as they were in the social insurance version: that they seek to find in insurance the qualities of sanity, organisation, attention to empirical research, and foresight which are lacking from orthodox tort theory. The aim is to rule out patchiness and unproductive exercises in blaming, and effectively to achieve the taming of risk.[17] At the same time, there is concern with distributive fairness, and especially the avoidance of 'regressive' tendencies. But on some accounts, modern insurance practice is the antithesis of universality, foresight, and distributive fairness. It is claimed that it rests upon surveillance, differentiation, and exclusion. This can be clearly illustrated by the double life of risk in governmentality theory, from the smooth surface of Simon's risk society, to the individualised and fragmented image of neo-liberal perceptions of risk. The 'own two feet' philosophy could thus end up in conflict with the argument which has begun to be used in partnership with it, namely that first party insurance operates more fairly. But I should add that I do not think that the contractual analogy employed by certain insurance theorists falls into quite the same trap, though Stapleton portrays it as part of the 'individual

[17] This ambition may be becoming increasingly difficult to satisfy. Prediction of risks by actuarial agencies is in some contexts becoming more problematic as risks emerge which could not be analysed on the basis of claims history. The extent of asbestos-related insurance claims offers an example.

responsibility' ideology. Rather, the contractual analogy shows a mixed interest in verification of solutions through individual preference, together with a faith in rational planning. This is a philosophically complex but quite familiar mix in liberal legal theory, as should become more obvious in chapter 5.

3. Contractual Alternatives

There are many potential roles for the law of contract in respect of allocation. When contrasted with tort law, at least as interpreted by the responsibility theories below, contractual solutions have a certain amount in common with the insurance approaches to the problem of accidental losses. To some extent, contract and insurance are genuinely and very simply linked. The 'mutuality' of the common risk pool is often, where insurance is commercially supplied, secured and defined through contract.

For the moment, I am going to concentrate on the analysis of one 'contractual alternative' to tort law in responding to products liability, in the version proposed by Jules Coleman in *Risks and Wrongs*.[18] One reason for doing this is that the theoretical basis of Coleman's contractual solution lies not in reasonableness but in 'rationality'. It is underpinned by a theory of rational choice. In this sense, and because of the links to insurance approaches, it provides a distinctive bridge between the present chapter and the ones that follow.

But there are also close links between the 'tort and insurance' issues raised above, and the contractual alternative. Some proponents of first party insurance and of the reform of tort law have used contractual analogies to explain that tort awards are too high and that the costs of the tort system would not be chosen by individuals who were given a free choice. Stapleton has interpreted this to mean that these theorists actually treat the parties as being in a contractual relationship, and that this is an erroneous assumption. But this seems to take the contract

[18] J Coleman, *Risks and Wrongs* (Cambridge, CUP, 1992) 407–29.

analogy too literally. For example, where the analogy is used to discuss an alternative approach to products liability cases, Stapleton suggests that there is a separate 'class' of non-purchasing consumers, who are clearly and paradigmatically covered by *Donoghue v Stevenson* tort liability but who would be excluded from the contractual solutions. She argues that this 'class' of non-contracting consumers was enriched by tort law, and that a move to contractual solutions would therefore be distributively unfair, because it would shift wealth from them to producers. But this misconstrues the point.

First, 'non-contracting consumers' do not, on the whole, constitute a separate class of people, though there may be some who consume more than they purchase. Generally speaking, and subject to specialised groups of consumers who never enter into contracts, there are only consumers who contract on some occasions and on others consume products they have not themselves paid for. Stapleton's definition is again framed by hindsight and relates to individual events. If looking prospectively at safety arrangements, it is excusable to make general points about 'consumers' as a group nearly all of whom at some point deal with producers through contract and certainly feel the impact of product pricing and availability.

Secondly, Stapleton does not fully appreciate that the contract argument can survive in a *hypothetical* form. Given that we can treat consumers as a whole as having a broadly contract-like relationship with producers both in terms of common interests and competition between interests, we can move on to imagine what would be the case if consumers and manufacturers *were* to bargain freely about product safety, compensation, and price. It is true of course that there are some philosophical assumptions involved in approaching the matter in this way—for example, that appropriate levels of safety and insurance are concerned with individual preferences and best approached through the idea of rational bargain—but these are not necessarily the same assumptions that Stapleton ascribes to them.

To some extent, Coleman shares a general view of tort law with Stapleton. In *Risks and Wrongs*, Coleman argues that tort law as a whole is not entirely continuous with contract. The law of contract he describes as being essentially concerned with markets (though not, in his view, centrally with efficiency). Tort law on the other hand is for the most part concerned with morals. Tort law requires certain parties to compensate other parties because they have a duty in justice to do so. The relevant form of justice is 'corrective justice', and the basis of liability is that there has been a wrongful loss.

Coleman argues, though, that products liability law can and should be approached separately from the main body of tort law. It is not necessarily the only area that can be separated from tort law in this way. Indeed, Coleman suggests that a given society may decide to deal with a whole range of losses through other mechanisms, such as a comprehensive state insurance scheme, and that if it does so there would simply be no claims in corrective justice at all. If there are no uncompensated losses, then there are no wrongful losses.[19] But in respect of products liability law, Coleman suggests that there are good reasons for proposing that the liability rules be modelled on contract, rather than on the form of corrective justice which he holds to be typical of tort law.

One of these reasons is the uncertainty of the present law; another is the over-exposure of manufacturers to liability and the consequent effects on manufacturing in the United States. But Coleman also suggests that the relationship between consumers and manufacturers is such that a contractual alternative is particularly appropriate. Consumers and manufacturers are often in a contractual relationship or something close to it. Many consumers are also purchasers, and it is purchasers who pay both for investments in safety and for insurance premiums indirectly, through the price of products.

As far as Coleman is concerned, these factors justify approaching product safety issues in a contract-like way. Even

---

[19] This overlooks the element in wrongful losses which is not recovered under insurance schemes, since insurance typically seeks to provide financial security, not full compensation.

though Coleman sees no necessary connection between contract and efficiency, he interprets contract as concerned with making arrangements in a prospective way. Contract, according to Coleman, is about coordination for mutual advantage. The similarity between insurance and contract in this respect should be obvious. That there may also be certain differences is discussed in the final section of this chapter, below.

The real problems arise when the consumer and manufacturer have not in fact specified what the allocation of safety risks will be. This may be because there is no actual contract, or because there was no negotiation over safety terms. Here, liability rules will most likely be needed to supplement real contracts. However, Coleman suggests that it is best for these to be based on the type of rationality normally associated with contract, rather than on tort, as is the current situation.

Coleman's method is interesting in itself. He is concerned not with the reasonable person tests familiar from negligence law, but with a solution which 'conforms to the outcomes of a rational contracting process'. Because the contracting process will be notional rather than actual, Coleman has to argue that we can specify what rational parties would agree to do about allocation of the relevant risks, if they had been in a position to negotiate. In arguing that we can specify this sort of thing, prospective allocation of risks is made to be a matter of rationality, combined with an observation about the common pattern of people's preferences concerning security and safety.

Coleman applies this method to two issues. He asks how much *insurance* rational consumers would wish to pay for in relation to their use of products; and how much *safety* they would wish to purchase.

So far as insurance is concerned, Coleman argues that rational consumers would not wish to pay for insurance to cover non-pecuniary losses (such as pain and suffering), but would only purchase insurance to cover pecuniary losses (such as lost earnings). The 'evidence' for this is that consumers do not purchase insurance cover for non-pecuniary losses in any other aspect of insurance. Indeed commercial insurers do not offer such cover, and Coleman is willing to assume that this illustrates lack of demand. The usual explanation for this preference on the part of consumers is 'marginal utility'. This is, in effect, a way of approaching risk aversion: this time, extra security (in the form of insurance payments) is less highly valued towards the top of the range, as more security is attained. People will therefore dedicate resources to providing a basic level of cover; but they will not choose to pay for a total reimbursement of all sums lost. Coleman claims that replacement of pecuniary losses is the sort of insurance required by most people to make the existence of the risk tolerable, or to make it acceptable to run the risk. Any more is not worth paying for. The contractual analysis therefore gives a reason for capping the damages available in product liability cases.

So far as risk reduction is concerned, Coleman suggests that the question is how much risk reduction rational consumers would want. Here, I think, it is particularly difficult to suggest that 'rationality' can provide a clear answer. In the case of insurance, the argument against non-pecuniary losses was based above all on observation of consumer behaviour, which was then explicable in terms of risk aversion. There was some evidence to go on, however debateable. Here however there is no such observed behaviour to report. Coleman suggests that the rational contractor would select a level of safety that is efficient—that is, the amount of total investment in safety would not exceed the amount of the total prospective losses.

But it is not at all clear that this efficiency standard would be the one selected by a group of individual contractors. It is a standard which seeks to maximise welfare across the board, and embodies one form of *collective* (not individual) rationality. Any individual risk-taker (ie, consumer negotiating purchase of the product, including price) would surely wish to compare their share of the cost of safety with the possible loss to them in the light of probabilities. They might well be prepared to 'over-invest' in safety, from the perspective of the efficiency standard. There would be nothing irrational or unfamiliar about this. The over-investment in safety is based on exactly the same reasoning as the whole institution of private insurance. Risk aversion is what makes insurance work, because it means that the fund should remain in surplus, bar unexpected events. But it also points away from an aggregate efficiency solution.

I think Coleman's contractual analysis of product liability does indeed have certain advantages over the tort analysis of the same issue. In particular, the *ex ante* form of contract, like all insurance mechanisms, draws attention to the fact that consumers do, at least in part, pay both for safety and for insurance through the price of products (and through general taxation and legal fees to support tort law in operation). The *ex post* form of tort law tends to lead us to forget this. The contractual analysis also draws attention to the fact that if consumers wish to benefit both from a range of products, and from an acceptable level of safety, then there are compromises to be made. Furthermore, it focuses the mind on the fact that safety is never total.

On the other hand, there are important problems or limitations. One is that the model depends on the existence of identifiable rational terms for a contract—a rational level of safety at an appropriate price, and with rationally acceptable insurance arrangements. There are problems here with disagreement about safety and about safety efforts. I have suggested that within Coleman's approach, we would at least need to recognise that consumers will be inclined to purchase more than the efficient level of safety, and that this is not irrational. In other words, I think that his contract model gives us a reason for reaching a different conclusion from the economic efficiency model. Whether we could say, if this was right, what a rational level of investment of safety would be for each individual consumer is far more controversial.

Finally, it should be pointed out that the level of safety that consumers prefer to purchase, if they are contracting, is not necessarily going to be a good guide to the best level of safety and risk generally. Some would say it is the best guide, because it is only when people have to give up something else in order to purchase safety that they put their minds to the question of what safety means to them. My point is that the level of insurance cover we would require within a contract to purchase goods does not necessarily reveal much information about our attitude to risk and safety more generally. It does not tell us what range of goods we would like to have on offer, for example. Issues of this sort are returned to in chapter 6.

There is a further point, which would become relevant in any instance in which it is implied that safety is genuinely a matter to be negotiated by potential victims. That is, that potential victims frequently have little opportunity to *discover* what the relevant risks associated with products actually are. The assumption of full knowledge is unrealistic. This underlines the need for a 'hypothetical' rather than an 'actual' contract solution. When read appropriately, the hypothetical solution does not lead to victim responsibility. It leads to some reduction in the level of damages or compensation; but it does not necessarily imply that people will be able to decide alone and for themselves what the ideal contract should specify. There are strong parallels with the 'insurance thought experiment' employed by Ronald Dworkin and explored in chapter 5 below. This too requires a debateable predictability or 'rationality' in risk and security preferences, in order to support a 'just' arrangement based on an imagined fair scenario. Like Coleman's solution, it is not based on the messy reality of actual consumer or insurance decisions. It is based on verification of solutions through appeal to personal preferences. These in turn are supposed to be predictable, and regular.

4. Risks versus Uncertainties?

Recently, Pat O'Malley has argued that too much attention has been given to the idea of 'risk', and not enough to the idea of 'uncertainty', in the governmentality literature.[20] He has illustrated this by reference to the evolution of the law of contract, and has claimed in particular that the 'subject' of contract law is

[20] P O'Malley, 'Uncertain Subjects: Risk, Liberalism and Contract' (2000) 29 *Economy and Society* 460.

above all an *entrepreneurial* individual. The common sense judgments of this subject are based on foreseeability rather than on calculation of probabilities. This in turn is said to mirror the influence of laissez-faire economic theory, which historically developed over the period during which this shift was achieved, and whose effect was to relegate expert analysis to a minor role.[21] A key moment in the evolution of this 'uncertain subject' is found, for example, in the development of 'expectation damages'. These are said to reflect the role of goods as being identified with profit potential, and thus to identify legal subjects as speculators.

To some extent, this thesis could be seen as essentially part of an internal debate within 'governmentality' theory, which O'Malley has claimed elsewhere is too quick to identify all references to risk with ideas of statistical regularity, expert governance, and evasion of issues relating to responsibility. I have already agreed that uses of 'risk' in respect of law have been too readily identified with this kind of regularity/expert-driven solution, and that this may in some respects lead to mistaken portrayals of legal theory. Feeley and Simon's description of tort law as 'actuarial' was an illustration of this. Indeed, O'Malley's thesis could be taken to provide evidence for the general point that individual agency is beginning to be taken more seriously as a theme in 'risk' theory. O'Malley, however, differs from my analysis in treating ideas about 'common sense', 'foreseeability', and speculative legal subjects as marking departures from thinking in terms of risk. I take a more flexible approach to what is involved in the idea of risk, and this is partly because I suggest that an 'agent-centred' idea about the future (including transformation of the future, which is the hallmark of the entrepreneurial individual) was involved in discussions about risk from

---

[21] Alternatively, it could be that courts tended not to understand risk in any technical sense, and were reflecting the 'everyday' language simply because this was their experience. Commercial law–especially contract law–is adaptable to the context in which it operates, perhaps more than it is adaptable to trends in political philosophy.

the very start. Certainly, a refusal to engage in actuarial and statistical approaches to risk makes this clearer, but in my terminology (and that of legal theory) it does not take us 'outside' risk.

In fact, O'Malley's analysis should alert us to some very important variations in the way that the role of the individual agent is handled, even within a broadly agent-centred, non-statistical approach to risk. In some respects, the idea of an 'entrepreneurial' agent, who arranges their affairs so as to change the future to their own perceived advantage, is present both in the liberal approaches I consider in this chapter (Coleman) and in chapters 4 and 5 below, and in the kind of neo-liberalism referred to by O'Malley. However, the liberal theories introduce some ideas about the predictability of these agents' preferences and choices, in order to be able to 'second guess' their choices and thereby, in effect, to propose right answers on *their* authority.

For example, Coleman and Dworkin both proceed on the basis that individual preference is the key to appropriate levels of safety/security, and in Dworkin's case in particular this is associated with an idea of life-planning and 'active' definition of the value of resources which is passingly similar to the contractual history recounted by O'Malley.

But even so, assumptions abound concerning the rationality of agents in their maximisation of (admittedly personal) preferences, and there is a large assumption of regularity in certain aspects of those preferences, relating particularly to safety and security. These are modelled on *what people typically want*, and how they are *thought* typically to respond to 'risk'. This in turn is drawn from models constructed by economic decision-theory. Perhaps above all, agents in both Coleman's contractual approach to product safety and Dworkin's insurance approach to equality are protected by the hypothetical nature of the respective exercises. This is one reason why these are not exercises in 'victim responsibility', nor are they neo-liberal accounts of the way that individuals must face an uncertain future armed only with the resources of whatever present they happen to inhabit. They are idealised, hypothetical accounts, which attempt strict demarcation in the roles of rationality and preference.

4

Risks, Outcomes, and Personal Responsibility

Opposition to the 'tort-as-insurance' approach investigated in chapter 3 centred on the view that accidents or misfortunes are not the responsibility of the general class of victims. Instead, it is fairer if the costs of making good accidental damage (as opposed to merely alleviating its effects) lies with the creator of risks. Those who opposed 'tort-as-insurance' on this sort of basis thought that departures from 'creator responsibility' were premised on a particular ideological viewpoint, and perhaps on 'victim responsibility' or an 'own two feet' mentality. I queried whether the 'tort-as-insurance' theories were genuinely based on victim responsibility, but agreed with the critics of these insurance approaches that their authors were at least incautious about their possible implications in terms of victim responsibility.

In this chapter, I turn to the apparent alternative or 'default' position, that responsibility for making good certain misfortunes fairly lies with the person or class of people who created that misfortune. Although Stapleton, for example, argues that fully socialised risk is also an alternative, she proposes that to relieve risk-creators of the burden of liability/insurance would be to enrich the class of injurers, and to remove from them a burden that is fairly placed at least partly with them.[1]

---

[1] It remains ambiguous whether her observations are intended to cover all 'risks', or only 'negligent' risks, and if the latter how negligence should be defined. See J Stapleton, 'Tort, Insurance and Ideology' (1995) 58 *Modern Law Review* 839. There she refers to a 'modern moral consensus' that protection against physical harms does not need to be bargained for, 'at least if carelessly caused by the defendant's positive act'.

We will focus particularly on two attempts to explain responsibility for misfortunes resulting from actions or omissions. The first is Honoré's theory turning on 'outcome responsibility', the second is Ripstein's account of responsibility for misfortune. It is important that both of these take very seriously the idea of 'outcomes', which is to say that they concentrate on concrete harms rather than on risk-taking in the abstract. Indeed 'risk' is introduced in these theories partly in order to justify attribution of those outcomes back to the actor. They both divorce the idea of 'responsibility' from any idea of 'culpability', even though Ripstein's account turns on 'reasonableness'. Ripstein explains that this is an idea of reasonableness which is not concerned with states of mind but with the quality and effects of action, and with the 'risks' brought about by those actions.

In both cases, I think that 'risk' is not just part of the chosen language of the theories, but is absolutely central to their structure. But equally, that idea is under-analysed in each case. Risk receives some explanation in Honoré's theory, though this still leaves large questions unanswered. It is left more obscure in Ripstein's theory, and in a sense becomes more obscure with further reflection. I suspect both authors proceed as though the implications of 'taking a risk' are obvious. For Honoré, this is even (in a sophisticated sense) part of his theory. That the implications of 'risk' are far from obvious should be clear by now. But as we unpack the implications of risk-taking just a little with respect to its use in these two specific theories, we will see that the liberal philosophy of action and responsibility on which at least the first of these theories draws makes the idea more problematic in moral terms than the theories allow for. Even more seriously, both theories (but particularly Ripstein's) neglect the direct overlap between their own concerns about action, uncertainty, and the balance between liberty and security, and the possibilities for dealing with *precisely* those concerns through a notion of insurance treated as an outcrop of decision-making or agency.[2] To raise questions about insurance is not to 'change

[2] The possibilities for treating insurance in this way are explored in relation to Dworkin's theory of equality in ch 5 below.

the subject' of these theories, but to engage directly with the issues that they raise.

In both these theories then, the authors seek to explain 'responsibility' in contrast both to culpability, and to 'insurance'. But I will suggest that in their combination of concerns with action, outcomes, and agency, neither approach is capable of resisting the pull towards insurance.

1. Tony Honoré: Actions as Bets

Tony Honoré has made extensive reference to 'risk' in developing his theory of personal responsibility for outcomes. It is interesting that Honoré associates all action, through the idea of risk-taking, quite explicitly with gambling. Honoré does not mean to compare life too directly with a game of chance. But despite recent doubts on the part of the author as to whether he should have used the analogy in the first place,[3] I suggest that it has more than superficial importance. Honoré implies that to act is in a sense to bet, and that we have a special relationship with the 'outcomes' of our bets.

The reason why acting (or in some cases, omitting to act[4]) is treated as similar to betting is that we do not know precisely how events will unfold following our action. We do not know for sure what effects our acts will have, good or bad. It is important that Honoré is here referring not just to material gains or losses on the part of the actor, but also to *moral* consequences, and general 'credit or discredit' that the agent may enjoy or incur. Honoré claims that 'outcome responsibility' is the most basic

[3] T Honoré, 'Appreciations and Responses' in P Cane and J Gardner (eds), *Relating to Responsibility* (Oxford, Hart Publishing, 2001) 225–26.

[4] According to Honoré, failures to act may in some circumstances be treated as equivalent to actions, and are then referred to as 'omissions'. Broadly, 'omissions' are not-doings where there is some relevant reason to expect us to act: T Honoré, 'Are Omissions Less Culpable?', printed as ch 3 of T Honoré, *Responsibility and Fault* (Oxford, Hart Publishing, 1999) 41. Readers should understand omissions in Honoré's sense to be included in all references to action in this chapter.

form of responsibility actually practised in law and elsewhere in our lives. Those of us who are capable of agency may, without unfairness, be held responsible for the outcomes of our actions, whether those outcomes be good or bad. Indeed, we *should* be so responsible, because of the implications for agency.[5]

Honoré does not argue that it is essential to outcome responsibility that we should have chosen to take a specific risk in any calculated and *literal* sense. In fact, he does not enter into discussion of the thought processes that might lie behind the 'betting' process, although he does use the vocabulary of 'choice' and of decision-making. It is more important in Honoré's terms that we come to own the outcomes of our actions because we have capacity as responsible agents. Having this capacity makes all actions into risk-taking, *because* that is the nature of actions in general. The strongest argument for outcome responsibility, according to Honoré, is that 'it is central to the identity and character of the agent'.[6] Without responsibility for outcomes, we would scarcely be persons, having 'decided nothing and done nothing'.[7] We are defined largely through the impact of our interventions in the world, and so we all *need* to be regarded as outcome-responsible.[8]

Outcome responsibility as it is described by Honoré is thus necessary because it is a vindication of agency. Without it, there would be surrender to 'determinism'. Honoré does not say so but the identification of statistical regularity and predictability in human affairs, which was so important for most of the 'insurance' and/or contract approaches to tort law, may be casting a shadow here. Outcome responsibility could be seen as directly opposed to 'social physics'.

[5] This does not however mean that we should necessarily be legally liable: Honoré explains that further justification is needed for this.

[6] T Honoré, *Responsibility and Fault* (Oxford, Hart Publishing, 1999) 10.

[7] T Honoré, 'Responsibility and Luck' in T Honoré, *Responsibility and Fault* (Oxford, Hart Publishing, 1999) 29.

[8] See also Nagel's argument, in respect of moral luck, that we cannot regard our actions as merely 'parts of the world': 'we are unable to operate with such a view, for it leaves us with no one to be', T Nagel, *Mortal Questions* (Cambridge, CUP, 1979) 38.

In summary, Honoré does not assume that we are all constantly engaged in a literal computation of the risks of action and inaction, and the likely consequences to ourselves in terms of praise, blame, or liability. But he assumes that the idea of a 'risk' is a sufficiently familiar one to be relied upon in describing as legitimate the attribution of effects to us as agents. To an extent, he adds the language of 'risk' and gambling to the existing accounts of 'moral luck'. I will return to this below.

The distinction between Honoré's theory, and libertarian theories of tort law, appears quite subtle, but can be used to emphasise the important role of agency, and of risk, in his account. The libertarian model of strict liability has been taken to propose that anyone whose actions caused interference with the rights of others should be liable for making good the interference in question.[9] On the victim's side, the interests protected are classically defined in terms of rights analogous to property rights. On the side of the 'perpetrator', the justification for liability is that damage (to protected interests) flowed from an action chosen by the defendant. Libertarian theorists alleged that this was an expression of individual liberty because, they supposed, there is a choice over whether to act at all, and especially over whether to act so as to create risks. This supposition is revealed to be false if we bear in mind that all actions and even lack of activity contribute to creation of risks. Lack of action, if kept up for long, also imposes considerable burden on others.[10] The whole libertarian aspect of libertarian theory is in doubt, because it is not possible altogether to avoid contributing to risks. There is no escaping the creation of risks to some level.

[9] A Ripstein, *Equality, Responsibility and the Law* (Cambridge, CUP, 1999) 32–47; S Perry, 'Honoré on Responsibility for Outcomes' in P Cane and J Gardner (eds), *Relating to Responsibility* (Oxford, Hart Publishing, 2001) 69, and S Perry, 'Responsibility for Outcomes, Risk, and the Law of Torts' in G Postema (ed), *Philosophy and the Law of Torts* (Cambridge, CUP, 2001). Both authors comment specifically on Richard Epstein's theory of strict liability.

[10] See S Perry, 'Responsibility for Outcomes, Risk, and the Law of Torts', n 9 above, p 86.

Creation of risk being unavoidable, strict liability for the effects of risks would not seem to respect individual freedom in the libertarians' sense after all. For Honoré however, the unavoidability of creating risk to some level is not a problem, it is in effect part of the solution. We take it for granted that we are risk-creators, and that risk-taking is inherent to action and certain types of inaction. Furthermore, we expect that we will be held in some way responsible for the consequences of our actions, because our identity and status are both understood in terms of our 'effects in the world'. Thus Honoré's main focus is on identity and agency, not on liberty. Although he uses the language of 'choice' to describe the decision to enter into a course of action, for example, it is not absence of constraint nor the optional nature of duties to others which he brings into issue, so much as the power of self-definition.

This is the way that Honoré escapes the trap set for the libertarians. The inescapability of risk-taking is not a problem which leads us to see responsibility as an infringement of our freedom; on the contrary, it means that risk-taking becomes an inherent feature of our perception of being a person. Being a person requires agency: agency requires responsibility for outcomes. The outcomes we create define our identity. This is why it seems likely that in a deep sense Honoré was being true to central claims of his theory when he said that we are all gamblers.

When stripped down to basics, Honoré's argument for outcome responsibility appears somewhat circular: we must be responsible because we need to think we are responsible or give up on agency and identity. But this circularity does not necessarily deprive his argument of its force. Recalling Jonathan Simon's doubts about 'limited liability' in risk society,[11]

---

[11] J Simon, 'The Emergence of a Risk Society: Insurance, Law and the State' (1987) 95 *Socialist Law Review* 61-89, pp 83–85. Simon suggests that in an (imagined) 'limited liability' society, we would be relieved of the adverse consequences of our risk-taking in the same way that stock holders in corporations are relieved of massive losses by limited liability. He suggests that 'something in our subjectivity is repulsed' by this imagined scenario. But unlike Honoré, he

Honoré's reasons for outcome responsibility are based not on the needs or rights of injured persons, but on protecting the agency (recalling Simon's sovereignty) of individuals perceived as risk-takers.[12]

In a sense, we do have a direct choice about whether personhood and sovereignty will continue to be decisive, given the development of other ways of approaching misfortunes, and particularly the possibility of approaching them as 'events in the world'. Outcome responsibility, according to Honoré, helps us to retain our sense of what it means to act. It will be remembered that Ewald could also be interpreted as arguing that insurance leaves the individual free—it does not strike at the individual, but creates a form of solidarity which does not require close allegiance in the same way that previous forms of solidarity did. The liberal theory of outcome responsibility outlined by Honoré differs from Ewald's approach in that responsibility for risk here is positively concerned with self-definition, while the collective technology of risk was linked with negative freedom, or with *not* making demands on the individual. Simon shares a perception of risk and its operation with Ewald,[13] but emphasises that the individual may be side-lined by the socialisation of risk, precisely through the removal of responsibility for consequences and effects. We need to consider whether Honoré provides sufficient justification for outcome responsibility in general, or for its particular embodiment in liability law.

concludes that the utility of those practices that are leading us towards limited liability (such as social security) is irresistible despite this impulse. On Simon's view, it is practicality, not sensibility, that is the stronger force.

[12] This is true of outcome responsibility as such. In Honoré's account of corrective justice, there is (as one might expect) a greater emphasis on the rights of the injured party, and this is also present in the more recent discussion of 'intersubjectivity' and the basis of the objective standard of care: see pp 17–19 below.

[13] Simon, n 11 above, p 84: '[h]ooked into an integrated grid of risk assessment and security measures, the individual is free to act within their credit limits without the sanction of any of the communities that once might have laid claim to defining the self . . .'.

Questions from Moral Luck

As already mentioned above, somewhat similar issues were considered by Thomas Nagel in his essay on 'moral luck', and by other commentators on the same problem.[14] Like Honoré's approach, this philosophical literature contradicts any argument that on moral grounds, there should be liability for wrongful *risk-taking*, not dependent on the outcomes of the risks in question.[15] It supports the idea of responsibility for outcomes, despite the problem that this means judging on the basis of something other than the quality of 'the will' alone.[16]

Honoré's approach is to suggest that there should be liability for the outcomes of one's acts, because it is a normal part of acting to take risks, and a normal part of risk-taking to be accountable for the outcomes. But Honoré does not replicate the sense, in Nagel's essay, that this responsibility is deeply problematic. He seems content with the idea of risk-taking combined with a startling assumption (considered below) that the arrangement is not only true to us as agents, but also fair. Nagel, on the contrary, concludes that major obstacles to moral judgment are posed by the way that both circumstances and fate (the situation in which we must act, and the outcomes of our actions) each operate to circumscribe the real ambit of our wills. The alternative, by which we continue to believe that our effects in the world are actually our own, remains essential because otherwise

[14] T Nagel, 'Moral Luck', n 8 above. For further insights on this issue, see particularly B Williams, 'Moral Luck' in B Williams, *Moral Luck* (Cambridge, CUP, 1981).

[15] See, for example, C Schroeder, 'Causation, Compensation and Moral Responsibility' in D Owen (ed), *Philosophical Foundations of Tort Law* (Oxford, Clarendon Press, 1995) 347–85. Schroeder argues that causation (whereby an adverse outcome follows one's acts) is 'often fortuitous and thus morally arbitrary', and that its use to distinguish between liable and non-liable parties violates the moral requirement of equal treatment (p 349).

[16] See *ibid*, Schroeder's suggestion that on a Kantian approach, it is only differences in intention or will that should be relevant to moral judgment. Nagel too introduces the 'puzzle' of moral luck by reference to Kant's insistence that moral judgment should direct itself entirely to the quality of the 'will'.

we would in effect be 'argued out of existence'. What is at stake is the idea of the active self. Again Honoré does not say so explicitly, but the 'gambling' device that he refers to is indeed closely related to the attempt to protect this 'active self', which was so clearly supported by early efforts to develop theories of decision-making building on probability theory.

Interestingly, Nagel also commented in his discussion of 'moral luck' that to hold people accountable for their acts without reference to their state of mind is akin to strict liability, and that strict liability 'may have its legal uses but is irrational as a moral position'. Honoré on the other hand implies that strict liability is the normal process of attribution in general, outside the law, *because* of the familiarity of risk-taking and its association with action. This he regards as the normal basis of *responsibility*, albeit separate from moral culpability as such. Instead, it is *legal* strict liability which, in Honoré's view, requires further justification. In other words, for sentiments of responsibility and attributions of blame to be accompanied by legal liability needs more than the agency idea.

Honoré does provide some further justifications for giving legal effect to outcome responsibility. One of these is general, which is to say that it is also supposed to support the moral aspect of such responsibility. This is the supposition that outcome responsibility operates, on balance, to our benefit. Another is specific to legal liability, because it concerns the distribution of concrete, material effects and costs. The latter is the principle of 'risk distributive justice', according to which it is fair to place the costs of outcomes with those individuals whose acts or decisions led to the adverse outcomes in question.

Unfortunately, the idea of 'risk distributive justice' is not especially well developed.[17] It holds, essentially, that the fairest way

[17] The relationship between outcome responsibility, corrective justice, and risk-distributive justice, is set out by Honoré in T Honoré, 'The Morality of Tort Law: Questions and Answers' in T Honoré, *Responsibility and Fault*, n 4 above, pp 78–81. Honoré emphasises here that distributive justice is not separable from nor inconsistent with outcome responsibility. The argument for legal liability (ie, for risk-distributive justice) is that it is fair 'to treat the agent as if he had made

to distribute risks is to allocate their effects to those who caused the damage; which is to say, those to whom we would normally attribute the losses. Ripstein attempts a similar type of argument at more length, about the fair distribution of the effects of risks. Discussion of Ripstein's idea of 'distributive' justice invoking risk will be found later in this chapter. For the moment, I shall say only that it is by no means self-evident that the fairest way to 'distribute' risks is to allocate their effects to someone who can be called the risk-creator. The 'alternative' solutions considered in chapter 3 will have a greater claim to be taken seriously, if the attempt to settle the question of *liability* (as opposed to responsibility) turns out to rest on a weak argument linking distribution with allocation as though this was 'self-evidently' fair. Immediately below, I examine some sources of unfairness in outcome responsibility. Then I turn to the relationship between outcome responsibility in general, and legal liability for outcomes.

The Balance of Benefits

Not only does Honoré argue that responsibility for outcomes is essential to the idea of the active self; he also argues that this principle operates fairly since agents of normal capacity will 'win more than they lose' on the basis of this principle. Since we are overall winners in terms of the general system of attaching credit and discredit, it is appropriate for us to 'take the rough with the smooth',[18] and to accept or expect discredit when we get things wrong, or in some other way end up with the wrong outcome. This idea has been widely criticised for its over-optimism, and

a bet on the outcome of his action' (p 79). The person who stands to gain should also take the risk of loss. Honoré returns to the question of justifying legal liability as a subset of outcome responsibility in *Relating to Responsibility*, n 3 above, especially at pp 223–26.

[18] The 'principle of taking the rough with the smooth' is treated by Honoré not only as possessing moral force, but even as encapsulating the principle of 'risk distributive justice': *Responsibility and Fault*, n 4 above, p 9. This should shed doubt on any effort to separate risk distributive justice decisively from outcome responsibility.

for its lack of supporting evidence or argument. Indeed it is optimistic and unsupported. But I will add one or two further questions here which are particularly related to our exploration of the idea of risk.

The first question is, why does Honoré believe, as many others do not, that we win more than we lose through the institution of outcome responsibility? Discussion on this point has tended to focus on 'shortcomers'. That is, commentators have often been concerned about the application of a general rule (or objective standard) to those who suffer from some trait or personality feature which limits their ability to avoid the consequences of moral discredit or legal liability. But I am more concerned to discover what lies behind Honoré's general confidence that those of *normal* capacity will be winners over all.

Is it really possible that Honoré can be claiming that there is in the nature of things a balance towards benefits, over the lives of *all* agents of normal capacity (who are, presumably, applying themselves reasonably earnestly to avoiding adverse consequences)?[19] One only has to reflect on the kinds of situation considered by Nagel to realise what would be so questionable about such an assumption. For example, Nagel raises the question of what would have been the state of mind of Jefferson, Franklin and Washington on their way to the scaffold, if the American revolution had not been a success and they had therefore fruitlessly brought about not only their own deaths but also those of many compatriots. Equally, what would have been the popular response to Chamberlain's appeasement of Hitler if the latter had suffered a heart attack shortly after invading the Sudetenland, and had never attacked the rest of Europe? Risk-taking by those of normal and indeed special capacity can have bad outcomes which are disproportionate to any of the 'benefits' of the same person's actions over a life, no matter how

[19] Unfortunately, there is ample evidence that Honoré does genuinely intend this meaning. For example, 'over a span of time more outcomes are likely to redound to our credit than to our debit, so that we are not permanently saddled with a losing ticket'. T Honoré, 'Responsibility and Luck' in T Honoré, *Responsibility and Fault* (Oxford, Hart Publishing, 1999) 26.

exemplary in both moral and material terms, that life may otherwise be. And we do not have to think in such large historical terms to see the same point. An accomplished surgeon who makes a fatal misjudgement may find all their life-saving work overshadowed by this one event, such is the response to losses as opposed to gains, or to error as opposed to routine excellence.

This most literal meaning for the 'balance of benefits' argument appears to rest on the supposition that the natural order of things will somehow even out in the end. There is no reason, in theory or in experience, for making such an assumption, and Honoré does not seek to provide such a reason. If we reject this particular supposition however, I think we are left with at least two possibilities. The first is that Honoré considers that agents of full capacity are so adept at decision-making that they can all make outcome responsibility work for them; the second is that he does not actually mean that benefits and burdens will really even out, in favour of benefits, across each life. Rather, he might mean that the institution of personal responsibility gives us the best *opportunities* of ending up in credit, over a life, compared with the alternatives, and that this is the case even if things do not turn out well for some agents of normal capacity.

The first possibility then is that agents of full capacity are so good at decision-making that they are able to make outcome responsibility work for them. Not only is it natural for agents to expect such responsibility, but they know how to act in order to make the most of it. If this is the true explanation, then Honoré would be introducing an idea which was not present in the basic statement of outcome responsibility. That is, that the approach which underlies outcome responsibility actually fits with our thought processes as we make the decision as to how to act and not to act. Gambling and risk-taking would cease to have their current role as *analogies* to action, and would become much more literal models for acting and deciding. Because we are expected to win on balance, this would further introduce the idea (an idea lacking from Nagel's account of moral luck, which had it that moral luck is a sort of necessary fiction which must

96

be retained in the teeth of more persuasive argument) that circumstances broadly conform with the laws of probability and are therefore negotiable by those with the right skills. I stop slightly short of suggesting that the 'right' skills here are skills of risk assessment and risk management, because Honoré also makes some reference to the alternative idea that agents of normal capacity have the fair opportunity to succeed because they are good at 'tracking standards',[20] for example, and learning what is expected or required.

In support of this interpretation, it is clear that Honoré does think that the idea of risk in itself operates naturally to *limit* liability to some extent. Thus the idea of outcome responsibility, explained in terms of risk, 'serves to foster a sense of identity because it does not stretch indefinitely into the future but enables each of us to claim for ourselves, or to share with a few others, outcomes of limited extent, whether successes or failures'.[21] I have already said that contemporary risks—the kinds of problems to which we currently have to apply risk methods—do not all have this neatly finite form.

In Nagel's consideration of moral luck, circumstances did not behave themselves and outcomes were palpably not fair, but he still retained one similar idea which was essential to the protection of moral judgment. That is, that moral judgments should not be entirely retrospective nor fickle enough to change with circumstance. For Nagel, an action cannot be morally right one day and wrong the next. Therefore, moral judgments made about actions under uncertainty are not retrospective, instead they are conditional. They can be made at the time of acting, and by any person (not just the actor). Such a person should be able to say: 'if this is the outcome, then your decision will have been right . . . if that, then it will have been wrong'. Such

---

[20] T Honoré, 'Appreciations and Responses', in P Cane and J Gardner (eds), *Relating to Responsibility* (Oxford, Hart Publishing, 2001) 219, at 225; Honoré derives this expression from P Pettit, 'The Capacity to Have Done Otherwise: An Agent-Centred View' in *Relating to Responsibility, ibid*, p 21.

[21] *Responsibility and Fault, ibid*, p 17.

judgments, for Nagel, count as 'timeless and objective'.[22] But this is a quite different argument from the suggestion that those of normal capacity should win more than they lose over time, and that *this* is essential for moral judgment.

What Nagel suggests is simply that chance is sufficiently determinate for people to have a go at hypothetical judgment before the event. Outcomes are 'foreseeable', in the sense that they can be imagined. Honoré would appear to be adding to this that with a moderate number of repeat performances (the number we each experience over a life), chance events will turn out right. Maybe this seeks to align the nature of personal decision-making (including a process of 'betting') with true regularity in events, *even* over a sufficiently small sample to be replicated in one life. This would not be plausible. The basic move towards insurance provision to cover accidents was premised on the much more respectable, but still increasingly vulnerable view that accidents will be predictable over an entire population year on year, but that they are *not* predictable over such a small sample of repetitions as would be constituted by a single life. No matter how good the skills of the gambler, proficient risk handling is not going to be able to 'cure' this problem. Honoré claims that 'risk and benefit go hand in hand'. But this is true only if there is some adequate mechanism to cover the outcome if one's chosen path does not lead to success. I think that Nagel is right, and that the majority of risky decisions in an individual life cannot be assumed to be like this.

The second alternative mentioned above was that Honoré does not truly intend to say that outcomes will turn out in favour of each actor of normal capacity over a life, provided only that those actors show the sort of know-how in negotiating risks (taking gambles) that one would expect. Instead, he might simply be saying that outcome responsibility is the fairest arrangement, since it gives us all the opportunity to be winners, and takes us all sufficiently seriously as 'actors in the world'. He might add

---

[22] Despite the reference to 'objectivity', I do not think this is intended to rule out moral disagreement.

that for most of us, most of the time, things will turn out for the best on balance through this arrangement. 'Risk and benefit go hand in hand',[23] but this time only for most of us. Honoré has recently come close to this formulation when dealing with the comments of Stephen Perry, who points out that the claim that outcome responsibility is beneficial to all is 'empirically, simply false'.[24] Here, Honoré says that we cannot pass as 'viable members of society' without exposing our behaviour and its outcome to assessment, and that 'outcome responsibility is a condition of the overall benefit that accrues to anyone who is treated as a rational person'. It is in this sense, which he describes as 'indirect', that outcome responsibility 'is not only inescapable but also a benefit'.

The idea of an 'indirect' sense in which outcome responsibility might be a benefit appears to make a break from the more literal balance of benefits over burdens which I have already questioned. However, Honoré in his reply to Perry only concedes that the literal balance of benefits over burdens fails in the case of 'life's perennial losers'—people who 'fail more than they succeed'. He suggests that we all 'know' people like this, and thus treats a tendency to fail as though it were a personal characteristic to be found only in a few individuals. This category of perennial losers is presumably different from the category of 'shortcomers' (those who fall short in some aspect of their abilities), but still represents an attempt to suggest that it is only some unusual individuals—this time the inexplicably accident-prone, or 'Mr Bumps' among us—who find that the benefits of outcome responsibility do not habitually exceed the burdens. This therefore does not meet the points about the general nature of consequences made above. Even if life is interpreted as operating on chance-like laws, or on the basis of rules and principles that we may in similar fashion negotiate through a sound method of decision-making, a single life does not offer enough

[23] T Honoré, 'Responsibility and Luck', n 19 above, p 26.
[24] S Perry, 'Honoré on Responsibility for Outcomes' in Cane and Gardner, n 20 above. Honoré's reply is at p 226.

'repeat plays' of the truly important decisions to justify any expectation that good and bad luck will even out.

But the main point is that even if we could interpret Honoré as making out a more general indirect case for outcome responsibility along the lines above, in place of the one that he applies only to shortcomers and losers, fairness would not be a notable aspect of the way that things turn out. The new argument, avoiding the charge of empirical falsehood, would be that the basic arrangements according to which responsibility is determined are fair, even though outcomes in individual cases and over individual lives often are not. We just have to accept those unfortunate instances for the sake of defending the basic arrangement. The difficulty is that this sort of concession would give us grounds on the basis of protection of individual agents, for wishing to ameliorate the *effects* of responsibility, where this is possible, or even to avoid responsibility as a component of our responses, if it is thought to be important to be fair to everyone. We come back to the idea that what is 'inescapable' as the basis for general judgments of responsibility need not be the basis for our approach to allocating or distributing concrete losses, if there is a fairer way of doing it. Indeed we might have good moral reasons for designing an alternative system for dealing with losses.

Outcome responsibility as the basis of a scheme for allocating losses is not 'inescapable' in the sense that Honoré uses that idea to describe outcome responsibility in general. Other potential solutions exist. Whereas Honoré argues, in effect, that responsibility is better than determinism and irresponsibility, he does not explain why responsibility, or 'risk distributive justice' founded upon responsibility, is better than other distributive approaches, such as those offered by the prospective mechanisms of insurance.

Outcome Responsibility and Liability for Consequences

At this point, for the sake of clarity, we should return to the question of how outcome responsibility is related to tort liability in Honoré's theory. It will be recalled that the question of how to allocate losses through tort liability was thought to depend upon distributive issues which were however related to the idea of risk-taking and responsibility. This was where we encountered 'risk distributive justice'. Recently, Honoré has appeared to accept at least some steps in the analysis of tort liability offered by Ripstein, whose theory as already mentioned differs in important respects from Honoré's. In particular, it offers no theory of 'agency', and purports to be wholly preoccupied with how to deal with the 'political' problem of how to allocate losses. Honoré accepts that the question which arises in tort law is not purely one of outcome responsibility, which concerns the issue of when we are judged to be *in some sense* responsible for outcomes, and is instead concerned with what Ripstein calls 'displacement responsibility', or the issue of when we should conclude that there is responsibility sufficient to justify shifting the loss from victim to perpetrator. He also concedes that the questions relevant to displacement responsibility are interpersonal ones. That is to say, they raise issues about the 'egalitarian' distribution of risks in tort law which will disallow us from varying the expectations we have of any given injurer on the basis of their lack of capacity.

Again, this latter point about the 'interpersonal' nature of tort law is presented as a justification for applying an objective standard of care, even to shortcomers. Nevertheless, it is extremely important that Honoré does not treat these justifications for tort liability as wholly separate from the theory of outcome responsibility. He continues to treat displacement responsibility as a 'subset' of outcome responsibility, and thus appears to differ from Ripstein on the question of how tort liability is ultimately justified.[25]

I suggest that attention to the issues raised in 'moral luck' about actions under uncertainty, combined with a little critical attention to the idea of 'risk-taking', lead us to conclude that the

[25] I say 'appears' because, as will be explained below, Ripstein's theory suffers from ambiguity over the possible meaning of 'risk ownership' in the absence of a theory of agency.

idea of responsibility is not itself sufficient to justify the *defence* of tort against good alternatives, and certainly not to go on the offensive and say without any further justification that those alternatives are unjustified simply because they are not based on responsibility. Neither would it be sufficient to seek a way out by saying that responsibility should be retained only for cases of negligence,[26] even if negligence is reinterpreted in terms of a more subjective standard of care than the one defended by both Honoré and Ripstein. Obviously, there is not space here to explore the relationship between negligence and strict liability. It will have to suffice to say that even *negligent* acts were included within Nagel's exploration of moral luck and the influence of circumstance. They were still problematic, because of issues relating to the degree of negligence relative to the size of adverse outcome; of inequality of circumstance leading to the final effects of negligence; and the influence of circumstances leading to the act of negligence. So even if negligence *is* to do with moral fault, as is neither obvious nor universally agreed, the effects of luck are still present.

It has long been noted that the 'objective' nature of the standard of care makes it hard to explain how negligence can properly be seen as a moral standard.[27] The questions surrounding 'moral luck' raise very similar questions, and theorists like Honoré have sought to articulate an idea of *responsibility* which is separate from *culpability*. But even if the objective fault standard can be convincingly defended in moral terms, this does not mean that the objective fault standard expresses the fairest solution to the question of accidents and how to distribute the losses in question. Looking beneath the surface, and keeping an eye on questions of risk-taking and of luck, Honoré's approach might lead us to conclude that responsibility judgments are often

---

[26] Neither Honoré nor Ripstein has any interest in doing this. Ripstein focuses on reasonableness in respect of interactions, so that his analysis is capable of extending both to negligence, and to strict liability.

[27] See for example P Atiyah, *Accidents, Compensation and the Law* (London, Weidenfeld, 1970) 453–58.

unfair in specific instances. We have also questioned his basis for arguing that they are fair over all.

2. Arthur Ripstein: Liberty and Security

Arthur Ripstein also treats risk-taking as central in explaining not only tort law, but also criminal law and certain aspects of distributive justice.[28] Ripstein does not suggest, as Honoré does, that we are prima facie responsible for the outcomes of our actions. Instead, he seeks justifications of responsibility within the specific coercive institutions of law. His theory, he says, is 'political'.

In both tort and distributive justice, he argues, there are practical questions which need to be answered. In tort, the problem concerns misfortunes—bad outcomes which have come about. Tort has to answer the question, whose misfortune was this? The same question is also central, he suggests, to distributive justice. In both tort and crime, Ripstein argues that there is only responsibility for outcomes if the 'fair terms of interaction' have been exceeded. These fair terms depend for their definition on the appropriate balance between liberty and security interests, which gives content to the idea of reasonableness. Liberty and security are interests that everyone has, so the balance is one of 'equality', not one that favours certain groups over others.

So far as tort is concerned, Ripstein's basic thesis seems initially simple. That is, we should all be required to bear the costs of our activities. In the case of tort, this means taking on the costs which result from our activities, so far as they impose risks on others. This Ripstein describes in terms of a 'Risk Rule'. This is the idea that 'those who expose others to risk are

[28] A Ripstein, *Equality, Responsibility and the Law* (Cambridge, CUP, 1999). In this chapter, now referred to as *ERL*. Page numbers in the text here refer to pages in *ERL*. Note that tort and distributive justice are thus treated as entirely separate regimes. Where crime is concerned, a completed crime is treated in *ERL* as 'intentional or reckless imposition of a wrongful risk plus harm within the risk' (221). Ripstein uses this definition to defend the legal position whereby attempts are treated differently from completed crimes.

responsible for the outcomes they cause' (p.65). If we ask why this should be the case, the immediate answer—the one offered by Ripstein in the course of introducing the 'Risk Rule'—is that 'those risks are in some important sense mine' (loc cit). Yet this 'ownership' idea is occasionally bolstered by the other, more political or practical reason with which Ripstein started—that the losses have occurred, and that the misfortune must lie somewhere. His argument is a combination of the two factors (a) the losses must lie somewhere, and (b) it is fairer if they lie with the owner of the risk.

This argument is problematic because the exact relationship between the two elements in the justification of liability—ownership, and the need to deal with misfortunes in a way that is fair to both parties—is awkward.[29] The supposition in (a), that the losses must lie somewhere, is in itself compatible with the general trend of this discussion, since it sets a political issue for tort to resolve, rather than consigning corrective justice to a self-contained and introspective category of its own. But the chosen solutions (what we might do with the losses) are limited and an important set of possibilities (relating to risk and insurance) is entirely overlooked, partly because of the focus on ownership, and partly because of the 'retrospective' vantage point adopted. Moreover, it is very difficult to discover any reasoned basis for the assertion in (b). I will save direct consideration of overlooked solutions for the time being, and deal immediately with the last point. This concerns Ripstein's assertion that we are 'in an important sense' the owners of the consequences of our risks, and that it is therefore fairer if losses are allocated to risk-takers.

Honoré, it will be remembered, offered a similar sort of argument about consequences, but that argument ultimately rested on the idea that agents have a special relationship with the out-

[29] Commenting on J Coleman and A Ripstein, 'Mischief and Misfortune' (1995) 41 *McGill Law Journal* 91–130, Stephen Perry has described the same difficulty in terms of a conflict between the political idea of 'allocation', and an apparently pre-political idea of 'ownership': S Perry, 'The Distributive Turn: Mischief, Misfortune, and Tort Law' in B Bix (ed), *Analyzing Law: New Essays in Legal Theory* (Oxford, Clarendon Press, 1998).

comes of their actions. We needed to be responsible, if we were to take agency seriously, and avoid slipping into determinism. Honoré had a particular view of what action was like—it was like risk-taking perceived in a particular (probably rather optimistic) way. But Ripstein says he has no underlying theory about agency or action. His approach is supposed to be political throughout. This leaves us with an awkward problem. If Ripstein has no theory of *agency* to offer, as Honoré did, where do we get the idea that we own the consequences of our risks, which seems to be the basis for allocating losses to us? Is this idea somehow to be gleaned from the idea of risk-taking itself?

The answer to the latter question is that the idea of ownership is not to be gleaned from the nature of risk-taking. On the contrary, the idea of 'risk-taking' is very selectively used by Ripstein to refer to the conclusion of a separate process, of reasoning about the 'fair terms of interaction' on specific occasions. The meaning of risk-taking is rather artificially constrained, and it tends to elude direct analysis. In respect of tort, the problems perhaps do not go to the very heart of Ripstein's theory, although they may certainly affect the over all judgment of it. In many respects, and if we ignore the use of the terminology of ownership, Ripstein has an attractive account of tort law. The key problem is with extension of somewhat idiosyncratic and misleading language when comparing tort with other solutions, and (part of the same point), with Ripstein's extension of very similar analysis to questions of distributive justice.

Initially, the Risk Rule (that 'those who expose others to risk are responsible for the outcomes they cause') seems both simple (subject to the causation issue) and very similar to Honoré's prescription. But even within one or two sentences, Ripstein has qualified what he means: ' . . . *if* I fail to exercise reasonable care, I expose others to risks' (p. 65, emphasis added). Now this 'if' at first glance seems misplaced in what appears to be a descriptive statement. Surely I could expose others to risk without failing to exercise reasonable care? Perhaps the conditional here is simply an oversight: Ripstein may simply be drawn

105

momentarily into the habit of presenting exposure to risk as wrongful in itself.

But it is not as simple as this. The truth is that Ripstein persistently adopts an idiosyncratic definition of what it is to take a risk, and what it means to say that someone has exposed another to risk. When he talks about risk-taking, he actually means, in effect, acting *subject to* the risk. This is not meant in a voluntary sense, nor in the sense that action is 'just like that', but in the sense that it is concluded by law that the risk lies with the actor. Ownership of risk is a conclusion, not a premise, of legal argument.

For Ripstein, only if the reasonableness standard is violated can a defendant in a tort case be said to have 'taken a risk' at all. 'Reasonableness' however is not about the taking of reasonable care in the course of a given activity, but about reasonableness judged in terms of whether the defendant's actions exceeded the 'fair terms of interaction'.[30] This judgment distinguishes between cases of liability and cases of no-liability. 'Reasonable risks . . . lie where they fall. Unreasonable risks belong to those who create them . . .' (p. 54). This is why 'belonging'—or ownership—is a conclusion of the enquiry.

There is a major difficulty with the choice of terminology here, because it leads Ripstein to treat reasonable risks as not being taken at all. Instead they 'merely arise'. This strains language more then a little in cases where the risk was run quite consciously, but reasonably so. To say that there is no liability or that the actor was not subject to the risk is one thing—it is relatively clear that this states a conclusion from argument. But to say that the risk 'merely arose' goes further, and appears to deny the influence of a deliberate agent. This selective terminology also allows Ripstein to gain rhetorical advantage from his misleadingly simple statement that people are responsible for the effects of the risks they 'take'.

---

[30] This has the advantage of being able to explain pockets of strict liability in terms of 'reasonableness'–of interaction, not of care.

106

So far as Ripstein's account of tort law is concerned, my reservations are these. First, Ripstein gains rhetorical advantage from the idea of 'ownership' of risks. In truth, the theory is about the allocation of losses. These losses or misfortunes are the practical problem which must be resolved by determining where they should lie. Ripstein tries to use the rhetoric of ownership to give tort law an implied moral advantage over other ways of dealing with such misfortunes, or to make the retrospective vantage point appear respectable. But second, there are also difficulties with the terminology of 'risk' itself. Ripstein uses the idea of 'risk-taking' to incorporate only unreasonable risks, which begs the question of whether reasonable risk-taking can exist, and what the correct destination of losses which flow from such risk-taking is supposed to be. It is almost as though Ripstein does not consider it possible to impose risks reasonably but consciously on others.

There is a third objection. This involves the question of alternative solutions. If 'ownership' is merely a conclusion, and a term into which we should not read too much,[31] what justification is there for approaching the relevant questions from within a tort framework in the first place? (And what reason is there for extending the same analysis to other questions, below?). Why are we even talking in terms of the 'fair terms of interaction'? The answer is not as innocent as Ripstein makes it sound. What he says is that tort law is about resolving the problem of misfortunes. These being a real problem, their burden must lie somewhere. But if we were genuinely concerned with the practical problem of misfortunes (and particularly with the protection of liberty and security), we could seek to deal with

[31] At *ERL*, p 54, Ripstein admits that his use of 'ownership' might be misleading. He says he means it in the same uncomplicated sense that swimmers, for example, are warned that they swim unattended at their own risk. He means merely to denote 'whose problem' the risk is. Again, ownership is a conclusion of argument, not a premise. But he does not post his own warning clearly enough. No such caveats are provided when making his broader statements about the basis of tort law in ownership of risks and of the costs of our activities.

these misfortunes prospectively. What reason can there be for looking back at events instead? It is possible that it is not so much the problem of misfortunes, as the definition of fair terms and of how we should live, that is the true preoccupation of Ripstein's analysis of tort law.[32]

Distributive Issues and Risk 'Ownership'

Distributive justice is linked closely with tort law in Ripstein's account. I suggest that the problems with his account of distributive justice stem partly from the same issues that we encountered in respect of tort law (above), but that they are even more significant in this different context. Thus while I do not disagree, in broad terms, that the justification of tort law depends on some issues which might be called 'distributive', Ripstein suggests that the problems of distributive justice are actually the same as those which he has already identified as arising in tort law. This is in a sense the opposite argument to the 'distributive' approaches visited in chapter 3: that answers to distributive questions can be found chiefly in issues of agent responsibility on specific occasions. Questions of distributive justice are thus made into questions of the choice between liberty and security on particular occasions, and the main preoccupation is with the divisions made on such occasions between mischief and misfortune.

Mischief and misfortune are terms introduced by Ripstein in respect of distributive justice. They appear to mirror the distinction in corrective justice between risks that are 'taken' and risks that 'just arise'. In chapter 8 of *Equality, Responsibility and the Law*, Ripstein considers the argument (which he attributes to Pashukanis) that the influence of circumstances is so great as to efface any meaningful distinction between what people do, and what merely happens. We are already broadly familiar with this possibility both from the discussion of moral luck, above, and from the general debate surrounding insurance and tort law, visited in chapter 3. But whereas Honoré identified the distinction

[32] This would be more in tune with Coleman's analysis in J Coleman, *Risks and Wrongs* (Cambridge, CUP, 1992) than Ripstein's presentation of his own analysis.

between what is done and what merely happens in the idea of acts and relevant omissions—above all, in agency and cause—Ripstein identifies the same distinction in terms of the division between 'mischiefs' and 'misfortunes'. Only unreasonable acts are treated as acts, and the outcomes of reasonable acts appear similar to things that merely happen. We can I think assume that this only applies to *adverse* outcomes—you may take the smooth but need not take the rough, so to speak. In opposition both to Honoré and to the philosophers of moral luck, Ripstein therefore seems willing to absolve actors altogether from the adverse effects of their own reasonable acts, at least so far as law is concerned. And, as explored above, the legal position seems to draw to some extent on a *pre*-political idea of ownership.

One of the most significant problems faced in respect of the 'distributive' aspect of Ripstein's approach arises from the basic method of the theory. Because Ripstein treats distributive questions, like tort, as turning on 'whose loss' a particular piece of misfortune is, he is led to treat that loss as a single indivisible unit. The range of questions about how we might justly or fairly deal with that loss is thus greatly restricted. Across the range of both tort and distributive justice, Ripstein considers only three possibilities for dealing with a loss. First, that the loss may be allocated to the risk-taker. Second, that it might be left to lie where it falls. Third, that it may be 'held in common'. With tort, we seem to have a straight choice only between the first two. Any mopping up of misfortunes which tort leaves where they fall will be done as a matter of distributive justice, and thus (we must assume) outside the tort system. Even at this point, Ripstein is already closing his eyes to the possibility that accidental losses, including those dealt with through the tort system, may actually be 'held in common' through the device of insurance, and that this might be justified by reference to the same interests—in liberty and security—that he discusses.

In other cases, outside tort, the situation is more complex. Many of the losses here will result from the actions or choices of the victim—these losses are self-imposed. It is not very clear how Ripstein responds to risks which are self-imposed, except that these too are to be judged 'normatively', in terms of a rea-sonableness standard. One reading of this is that losses which are self-imposed and where there is no unreasonableness in the acts of the agent are to be 'held in common', while those which are the product of unreasonableness on the part of the agent are generally to lie where they fall. However, the agent gets a second chance in the latter case, because losses must be held in common to the extent that they would otherwise deny the agent the possibility of participation on fair terms in future interac-tions. This is a 'bottom line' which illustrates the underlying importance of agency and choice in Ripstein's approach.

But Ripstein does not say very clearly what should happen to losses stemming from *reasonable* self-imposed risks, and this mir-rors his general silence on reasonable risks imposed on others. In respect of tort law, reasonable risks probably lay where they fell (thus closing the door on no-fault liability solutions).[33] In this different context, he might mean that the mirror-image applies—that is, that reasonable self-imposed risks, being reasonable, are not 'ours', and therefore ought to be held in common. But if Ripstein really means that all reasonable self-imposed risks are to be 'held in common' then there will be a great deal of redistribution securing a great many interests. And this leads us to a further problem.

It has already been said that Ripstein treats losses as indivisible and that, in tort, he tended to ignore the idea of loss-spreading through insurance. When it comes to issues of fair distribution, Ripstein introduces the idea of 'holding in com-mon', but gives no express attention to what 'holding in com-mon' would mean. The demands of justice come first, and the mechanism for providing what is required limps in a poor sec-ond. But the mechanism, in this instance, is enormously signif-icant. Because the idea of a 'loss' is generally discussed by Ripstein as an indivisible unit, we might assume that losses must be made good in full to satisfy the demands of distributive jus-tice. The effect would be staggering, with the security of all

[33] *ERL*, p 54.

interests, in wealth, health, or whatever, being made good through the common purse whenever there was a loss not attributable to someone's fault. This would amount to security *de luxe*. It would also make a call on everyone to secure even the most refined interests of the wealthiest. It would be hard to justify their lack of any obligation to insure themselves.

Perhaps then this is not what Ripstein has in mind. Perhaps he has in mind that this awkward category (within his theory) of losses stemming from *reasonable* self-imposed risks is not to be made good after all (unless and to the extent that the risks deny the fairness of future exchanges involving the victim of those losses). That however seems an equally implausible interpretation of Ripstein's theory, because the mischief-misfortune dichotomy (which, as explained above, he treats as central to distributive justice[34]) would not operate at all then in respect of self-imposed risks. Furthermore, such an approach would not to any great extent provide 'security' of existing interests, redistribution being limited to a 'base-line' of opportunity.

There is yet another alternative, which is that the question of how to treat self-imposed risks has nothing to do with reasonableness of *risk-taking*. Reasonableness may have a different role. The difficulty is that the only alternative offered is in the form of a very broad question: is it reasonable for the victim of misfortune to bear this particular loss?[35] We know that the answer to this question of reasonableness will not depend on the 'choices' of the unfortunate party, but other than that there is little indication of what the content of the test might be.

In the end, perhaps it does not much matter, because the problem goes deeper. In the case of self-imposed risks, there is no 'other party', only the risk-taker and the broader group. Whatever test Ripstein has in mind, he still poses us an either-or choice between 'liberty' and 'security'. If we treat the loss as

---

[34] *ERL* ch 8, and (generally) J Coleman, and A Ripstein, 'Mischief and Misfortune' (1995) 41 *McGill Law Journal* 91–130.

[35] This appears in *ERL*, p 268: 'they should bear only such costs as it is reasonable for them to bear, in the light of the interests of others'.

a single unit, then it must either lie where it falls, or somehow be foisted upon society at large.

The truth is, any reasonable system of distribution would have to compensate less than fully in the case of losses falling outside tort law (and arguably, if we accept the arguments based on insurance and/ or contract in chapter 3 above, within the traditional field of tort law too). Ripstein is not especially interested in what happens to those risks that 'just arise', because his main concern is with responsibility and defining its limits. He wants to know *which* losses should be treated as 'just arising', and assumes that Dworkin (who is discussed in the next chapter) has the same overriding interest, too, through his distinction between choices and circumstances.[36] Yet insurance constitutes a mechanism for sharing risks (and thereby losses) which is relevant on many levels to Ripstein's enquiry. It seeks to protect both liberty and security, it fills the void which 'holding in common' seems to throw open by suggesting how this could be done, and it also provides a further 'choice' for people wishing to act reasonably in respect of risks. Thus it is not just an alternative technical means of *distribution*, but an alternative avenue for thinking about responsibility. Given Ripstein's concern with actual losses, and with liberty and security, it does not seem possible to justify the exclusion of insurance from consideration. As such, its exclusion simply underlines the over-emphasis within his theory on individual responsibility of a particular kind.

We can take some steps now to flesh out what is missing in Ripstein's focus on past risk-taking as opposed to prospective risks, and his general silence on the question of insurance. Chapter 5 will open some new possibilities. Risk-based approaches to misfortunes associated with insurance, take a prospective approach to misfortunes and use risk in a forward-looking way to define the chances of a given category of person suffering a particular range of misfortunes. Ripstein looks retrospectively at misfortunes and uses 'risk' as a largely rhetorical device for designating the person to whom these misfortunes

[36] *ERL*, pp 278–84.

should be allocated. But distributive 'solutions' to the problem of accidents are built on a range of techniques which have historically transformed the way that societies respond to misfortune. In particular, the 'insurance' solution argues that in contributing in advance, people are not paying retrospectively for another's misfortune, but providing security against misfortune both for themselves and for others. In this sense it *exploits* uncertainty. Ripstein argues that 'holding in common' limits freedom by asking people to contribute to something that was not their responsibility.[37] But this misses the point. Distribution via insurance can be seen as typically concerned not so much with retrospective hand-outs as with prospective risk pooling and risk management. Looking at the risk prospectively may indeed change the way that we assess fairness, as Ewald suggests. Looked at this way, the payment to those suffering misfortune is a matter of entitlement based on mutuality, and the call upon others is a matter of right according to which they too would have had the same call in the same circumstances.

I do not mean to suggest that insurance attains its goals perfectly. In fact, in chapter 5 I shall explore some ways in which the philosophical transformations claimed to have been wrought by insurance are challenged at a deep level by contemporary developments. The point is that to apply an entirely backward-looking approach to risk in distributive questions is to miss the opportunity to protect *both* liberty *and* security, which was exactly the contribution of insurance on Ewald's analysis, but which may also have relevance within a more classically liberal, agent-based framework. Ewald overstated the conflict between liberalism and distributive issues, perhaps; but liberals like Ripstein tend to perpetuate the myths involved. Liberty and security are precisely the two interests which Ripstein seeks to balance case by case, but the offered solutions seem to do a poor job of securing either. Though insurance carries out its purposes

---

[37] *ERL*, p 271: though indemnification of a loss may, under loss spreading, impose only a 'trivial burden' on each individual, nevertheless 'being asked to bear even a share of some cost is a limitation on freedom'.

collectively, it is meant to achieve a balance between liberty and security for individuals, too. Both Coleman (above) and Dworkin (below) seek to demonstrate that rational actors would choose insurance solutions to the questions posed by uncertainty. Protection is modelled on what would be chosen in this way; thus such approaches are very different from 'victim responsibility', which would foist the responsibility for insurance onto those who may be at risk.

Ripstein's theory is not alone among liberal approaches in systematically understating the importance and the possibilities of actively distributive solutions. It is however a clear example, and I believe it is all the more obvious for expressing itself in the language of risk. I do not say that an approach based on 'risk' must by definition be prospective, or collective, nor that it cannot be agent-based. But Ripstein's own theory opens up the type of issues which beg the question of why individual agents would not choose the insurance 'compromise'. In the next chapter, I will consider among other approaches Dworkin's quintessentially liberal use of a hypothetical insurance market in tackling questions of equality and justice in distributions. I will say for now that I think Ripstein has misrepresented the focus of Dworkin's theory because of his own general assumption that questions of distribution come down to the definition of ownership and its limits.

3. The Changing Boundary Between Risks and Outcomes

Risks as Damage?

Among the questions about risk which have begun to affect tort law, one in particular relates back to aspects of the responsibility theories, above. This is the question of whether risks can be the proper basis of liability, independent of damage.

The usual argument in favour of liability for risk creation *per se* is simply that there is no morally defensible distinction between a defendant who wrongfully creates a risk but is lucky enough to create no damage, and a defendant who wrongfully creates a risk but is unlucky enough to create some damage.[38] But the arguments about moral luck, above, which were central to Honoré's interpretation of tort law, suggest that luck inescapably plays a role in moral judgments about responsibility. Thus, they suggest that distinctions between lucky and unlucky defendants must be defensible, because they are morally indispensable. I will not say anything further about those theories now, except to explain how the arguments of both Honoré and Ripstein contain their own reasons against imposing liability for risk-creation per se. In this instance, they are compatible with the answer from 'insurance'.

Reasons why risk is not damage

Honoré's theory depends on outcomes and their special link with actions. Part of Honoré's reasoning for outcome responsibility is that we can all expect to gain, on balance, from such a system of responsibility. This expectation of gain may either be material, or have more to do with credit and discredit. In general, good outcomes will outweigh bad outcomes, and this is essential to the fairness of the system of responsibility. I have already suggested, above, that this balance is doubtful. For now though, it should be pointed out that Honoré's argument from fairness also gives a reason against imposing liability merely for imposing risks, in the absence of any damage. If responsibility is imposed even in the absence of any bad outcomes, then within the terms of Honoré's theory, we upset any hope of achieving a positive balance within what he describes as the most familiar form of responsibility. We all create risks habitually, and liability for mere risks would turn us all into losers.

Ripstein's theory did not include any hypothesis about the balance of benefits and burdens. However, his theory too provides reasons against the imposition of liability for risks per se—this time explicitly.[39] His approach to tort law is premised on the

---

[38] See Schroeder, above n 15.
[39] *ERL* p 72–84.

existence of misfortunes. He says that it is really these misfortunes, rather than the existence of risks per se, which makes it necessary to adopt mechanisms for allocating and distributing losses including tort law. Tort law therefore deals with losses, which Ripstein discusses in terms of misfortunes. Ordinarily, if the defendant is lucky and does not cause damage, then potential victims are lucky too and do not suffer any. From this point of view, to create liability for the unintentional, even if wrongful, creation of risks would be to create more misfortunes. This would clearly be undesirable.

Within the framework of responsibility approaches, these reasons suggest that a move toward liability for creation of risks would be a move in the wrong direction. The idea of insurance leads to a similar conclusion, but even more decisively. In insurance, risks are shared and losses are made good from the common pool. Recovery for mere risks would therefore be simply incomprehensible, and losses and risks must be treated as separate categories. This makes it all the more significant if there is indeed pressure on the boundary between losses and risks.

The Nature of the Challenge

The dividing lines between risk and damage are becoming more difficult to draw, and in certain types of case the changing perception of risk has actually pushed the experience of risk exposure much closer to the experience of suffering damage. These cases may be relatively easy to incorporate, formally speaking, into corrective justice theory—we simply say that at some point, the risk has crystallised into actual damage, and at that point the case is properly one for the attention of the law of tort. The difficulty is that the balance of theories like Honoré's and Ripstein's may be upset if this means that more effects can be interpreted as 'outcomes' rather than as 'mere risks'. There could also be significant problems of uninsurability.

Varied examples can be provided of cases where 'being at risk' brings about suffering in itself. For example, having an enhanced 'risk' of developing a serious disease or other medical condition may affect prospects of insurance. Insurability is essential for full participation in many of the benefits of contemporary societies. The 'loss' here—uninsurability and its implications, such as exclusion—is a direct consequence of being at risk. Furthermore, the damage comes about because of the very prevalence of risk-based and actuarial techniques in many aspects of social organisation. Similarly, designation of a property as 'at risk'—whether from flooding, subsidence, or contamination of one sort or another—can directly affect its market value, because of the practice of risk-rating. Expanding information and *recognition* of risk alters the concrete impact of risk.

The most difficult cases to categorise perhaps are those where being at risk creates mental effects. This includes 'fear of cancer' cases, where individuals who learn that they have been exposed to carcinogenic substances may have their notional risk of developing cancer increased by some percentage, and seek compensation for the mental effects. One of the problems is with defining whether the fear in question is 'reasonable'. Some of these cases are highly contentious because there is only weak evidence for a causal link between exposure and disease at all, so evaluation of the 'damage' is deeply problematic. At the other extreme though are cases where certain individuals are subject to a much increased chance of contracting a condition, and this has tangible effects on their mental state. In the UK, damages have been awarded to individuals treated with inadequately screened human growth hormones, who are therefore at a greatly increased risk of contracting CJD.[40] These damages are for psychiatric effects stemming from the knowledge of potential disease, and not for the exposure to risk itself. And yet, it is

---

[40] *Newman v Secretary of State for Health (No 1)* (1996) 7 Med LR 309; (2000) 54 BMLR 8. Morland J's treatment of one particular group of claimants ((2000) 54 BMLR 95) was reversed on a different point, relating to the date of treatment and the finding of negligence, by the Court of Appeal: (2000) 54 BMLR 85; The Times, 20 December 1997. See M Mildred, 'The Human Growth Hormone (Creutzfeld-Jakob Disease) Litigation' [1998] *Journal of Personal Injury Law* 251–70; J O'Sullivan, 'Liability for Fear of Onset of Future Medical Conditions' (1999) 15 *Professional Negligence* 96–110.

awareness and experience of the risk—*not* materialisation of the risk, as we are used to debating it—which brings about the harm.

As suggested above, these well-defined cases of liability for the effects of being at risk do not depart from established principle, but adapt those principles to new fact situations. Nevertheless, they may lead to problems for outcome responsibility whether this is based on action or on wrongdoing. The habitual analysis of situations in terms of risk, and in some cases greater awareness of risks, means that the adverse effects of risk-taking are actually enhanced. This may occur through exclusion—whether from markets or from social security measures based on insurance—or through the mental suffering associated with knowledge of being 'at risk'.

Simply, this development is about multiplication in the *types* of outcomes which can be traced to action, and this effect is in turn enhanced by greater knowledge of and attention to 'risk'. Insurance may indeed undermine itself, as being 'at risk' is a continuing state which may lead to loss of insurability—and thus amount to concrete damage after all.[41] We should not overlook that the contours of the distinction between damage and abstract risk are therefore changing, and indeed that this alters the nature and implications of the idea of 'risk' itself. Clear thinking about risk, and its distinction from harm, is important, but so too is flexibility in defining this boundary.

We should particularly note the argument of Porat and Stein,[42] that we have entered a third and new phase in the evolution of tort doctrine. Following a period dominated by simple physical causation, the second phase they assert was marked by expression of liability in terms of 'wrongful exposure of another to risk of sustaining damage . . . and damage from the materialization of the risk'. This they suggest was based on the ability to exercise control over risks. For Porat and Stein, the new phase of tort law concerns damage that is untraceable to a particular

---

[41] See the discussion of potential exclusion from important aspects of well-being or security on the basis of uninsurability, in ch 5 below.

[42] A Porat and A Stein, *Tort Liability Under Uncertainty* (Oxford, OUP, 2001) 9.

risk-taker, or which is indivisible as between several risk-takers. This phase is therefore characterised by problems of proving causation, but they continue to suggest that wrongfulness and externalisation of risk are essential elements for liability.

The new phase is said to be made necessary partly by the evolution of a multiplicity of risks, and partly by inequality in the distribution of control over risks. These are changing social conditions to which tort needs to respond. The latter reason would indeed be part of the argument against first party insurance, since it implies that the risk-creator is the only person in the appropriate position to know and to control the risks in question; it also implies a decline in reciprocity of risks. These could actually be arguments for retaining tort and third party insurance solutions, if they can be sufficiently adapted, rather than moving to victim responsibility. Porat and Stein add a third reason, which is 'scarcity of information' concerning risks. As will be clearer in chapter 6, it is the explanatory or predictive power of information, more than its scarcity, that is in issue.

Porat and Stein set out an array of cases where the causal link between a known risk-creator and the particular damage has been unprovable in traditional terms. They illustrate that tort law has in many instances responded to such issues by adopting a probabilistic or statistical approach to proof of causation, in order to compensate victims of harms through awards against known risk-creators. Courts have, finally, embraced some elements of statistical and probabilistic method in seeking out sufficient evidence of 'materialization of risk'. It is the required evidence to justify the link between particular agent and particular effect, rather than the whole philosophical basis of responsibility, which is altered by these cases.[43] In part, this reflects the

---

[43] See the House of Lords decision in *Fairchild v Glenhaven Funeral Services Ltd* [2002] UKHL 22. Here, mesothelioma sufferers had worked for several employers each of whom had in breach of duty exposed them to asbestos dust. It is thought mesothelioma may be caused by a single exposure, but the risk of suffering it increases with length of exposure. As against each employer, the claimants could therefore establish no more than a statistical contribution to the risk of developing their condition. The House of Lords accepted that in these

statistical nature of knowledge claims, and the preponderance of research in statistical terms. But Porat and Stein also success-fully illustrate that as *risk itself* begins to affect lives more closely, so courts have sometimes been willing to align their methods to this new state of affairs.

circumstances, it was sufficient to prove that each defendant's breach of duty had materially increased the risk of contracting the disease, thus making possi-ble liability on the part of any of the employers.

5
Distributive Justice, Insurance and the Individual

The exploration in this chapter illustrates the general point that introducing a 'risk' discourse does not by itself determine one specific political or philosophical perspective. This is still the case, even if that risk discourse remains focused upon a single technique. In this instance, we pursue a particular interest in insurance, and especially in the relationship between insurance and distributive justice or fairness.

Culpitt has recently associated 'risk' in welfare discourse specifically with a neo-liberal perspective,[1] just as certain criminologists have associated risk with neo-liberalism in the sphere of crime control. For many in the English-speaking countries, this link seems obvious enough. Risk categories are taken to provide a way of differentiating between people; and insurance is seen to proceed on the basis of classification. On another view though, insurance is, through its pooling of risks, universalising. Indeed, as we saw in chapter 2, this has been described as the primary historical impact of insurance.[2] In this chapter, we

[1] I Culpitt, *Social Policy and Risk* (London, Sage, 1999).

[2] See also P Baldwin, *The Politics of Social Solidarity* (Cambridge, CUP, 1990) 1: 'Applying the instruments of social insurance . . . decisively advanced society's ability to treat each of its members equally. It did so, however, less by redistributing wealth than by reapportioning the costs of risk and mischance'. Within the UK, the welfare state has traditionally been seen as a primarily political rather than technical project, promoting equality and the elimination of need, rather than dealing technically with risks and their management. Even so, it is now increasingly common to see British writers describing the institutions of the welfare state in terms of insurance. N Barr, *The Welfare State as Piggy Bank* (Oxford, OUP, 2001) and Giddens, *The Third Way* (Cambridge, Polity

observe some very different accounts of welfare incorporating an insurance analysis, in order to review these possibilities.

First, there will be a return to legal liberalism, but this time in a different context. Here, we will explore Dworkin's attempt to use insurance as part of an egalitarian liberal approach to the fair distribution of resources. Dworkin's approach will be compared not only with the liberal responsibility theories of accidents (and more) outlined in chapter 4, but also with the other approaches to risk, distribution and welfare discussed in this chapter. Importantly, Dworkin links insurance with decision-making by individual agents. He focuses on a hypothetical decision about whether to insure, and provides a dimension lacking from the responsibility theories explored in chapter 4. I explained there why this dimension was needed. Second, we look more closely at some of the philosophical aspects of Ewald's 'insurance society' analysis, with particular reference to his argument that solidarity replaces responsibility as the paradigm of these societies. We will test the nature of the 'solidarity' seen in insurance, and ask how it relates to 'mutuality'. This prepares us for the third section, which explores some problems of collective risk management and considers the emergence of a new focus upon the individual. This suggests that the link between mutuality and solidarity is under pressure. But also, the question arises of whether it is right to describe recent developments less in terms of 'individualism' (which can claim to be among the philosophical foundations of liberalism), and more in terms of 'individualisation'.[3]

1. Egalitarian Individualism and Risk: Dworkin's Hypothetical Insurance Market

Dworkin has himself made connections—albeit fairly impressionistic ones—between his own exercises in liberal political

Press, 1998), each emphasise the insurance function of the welfare state and particularly its use 'over a life' by all including perhaps centrally the middle classes.

[3] 'Individualisation' is explained on pp 142–43 below.

philosophy, and the 'third way' politics which came to the fore in Britain and the United States in the late 1990s.[4] For Dworkin, the goal is to show how 'equality' and 'responsibility' are not opposed, but compatible virtues. This he supposes is consistent with the aim of 'third way' politicians to find a route between 'old' left and right positions.

Certainly, third way politics include an emphasis on the individual and in particular on personal responsibility. I would suggest however that the notion of 'responsibility' employed by Dworkin is rather different from the uses of that term encountered in the work of Giddens, for example. More obviously, it is also very different from the neo-liberal uses of responsibility which it might superficially be thought to resemble.

Neo-liberals and third way theorists tend to emphasise 'choice'. It is true that Dworkin too argues that 'choices' are important, and that the element of choice should make a difference to the way that we approach material inequality or need. There seem to be clear points of contact here with Giddens' suggestion (as an example) that many health risks should be treated differently because they are the product of life-style rather than pure 'chance'.[5] Nevertheless, I believe it would be a mistake to read Dworkin as saying that people should be 'stuck with' the consequences of their choices, on the basis that they are their own (an 'ownership' idea similar to Ripstein's), or on the basis that they are thereby responsible for their own suffering or 'make their own luck'. Rather, the central thrust of his argument is that *equality itself* can only be understood in terms of the values that people attach to different chances and opportunities. This preoccupation with the meaning of a core ethical term, rather than with adaptation to changed conditions, marks a major distinction between the liberal and 'third way' approaches. Above all perhaps, Dworkin's notion of responsibility for

---

[4] R Dworkin, 'Introduction: Does Equality Matter?' in R Dworkin, *Sovereign Virtue* (Cambridge, MA, Harvard University Press, 2000).

[5] Giddens, however, stops short of spelling out what implications follow from the 'choice' of lifestyle influencing health risks. Should there be individual responsibility, or social responsibility for altering lifestyles?

choices requires a level playing field, and thus remains more hypothetical than he sometimes admits.

The Auction and Initial Equality

Dworkin's essay 'Equality of Resources' begins with the design of an idealised 'auction', carried out on a desert island among immigrants in order to divide the shared resources of the community in an 'equal' way.[6] Each immigrant receives a certain number of 'clamshells' with which they will bid for the various resources.

However, it is important to note that the process of the auction itself is not the clinching factor for defining equality. The outcome is not considered equal *because it is the result of fair choice in a well-run auction*. That would genuinely be a question of holding people to their choices, given fair circumstances. Rather, the outcome is considered fair because each immigrant ends up with the 'bundle' of resources that they *actually prefer*, bearing in mind the opportunities foregone to secure these particular resources. This is a question of people's preferences dictating what is to be regarded as an 'equal' distribution, where the auction is merely a device for arriving at this distribution. True, the preference of each individual for their bundle is only relative: they do not prefer anyone else's bundle; but they do not necessarily have everything they would like to have either. The important thing is that the 'envy test' should be satisfied, by which no individual prefers another's bundle to their own. Evidence for saying that the envy test, rather than the fair process, is crucial is this: if the envy test is not satisfied, then the auction is rerun—and this continues until the test *is* satisfied.

The 'auction' process is however not a mere distraction. It is designed to illustrate that the contents of each individual's bundle of resources must be affected by the 'opportunity costs', to

[6] R Dworkin, 'Equality of Resources' in *Sovereign Virtue* (Cambridge, MA, Harvard University Press, 2000) 65–119 (now referred to as '*ER*'). Page references here are to the version printed as in this publication. However, the essay was initially published as 'What is Equality? Part 2: Equality of Resources' (1981) 10 *Philosophy and Public Affairs* 283–345).

others, of their holding those resources.[7] It concerns the themes of scarcity and coexistence, because it reminds us that anything we have will potentially be ours at the expense of someone else, *and therefore* of something else that we could have had ourselves. If we really had a choice, as people are assumed to have in the 'ideal' conditions of the desert island auction, that choice would nevertheless be limited in the sense that it would come at a price. 'To choose' means giving up some options in favour of others.

It will be remembered from chapter 4 that for Honoré, to act was to choose to take a risk, in the sense of taking the risk of its outcome. As explained below, when Dworkin discusses choice, he refers centrally to the chosen balance between security and opportunity. Through the insurance principle, this modifies even hypothetical outcome responsibility very significantly.

The Broader 'Project', Option Luck, and the Insurance Principle

Although the auction is not a mere sideshow, it is in a sense only a preface. The auction only supplies the core idea of how 'equality' should be recognised. The main 'Project'[8] is to determine what approach to distribution of resources in a functioning society will satisfy the demands of equality, while also respecting liberty. This question introduces a number of other dimensions, including those associated with an economy and employment, but most crucially for us it introduces the idea of the future and of various kinds of 'luck' over time. Because of different individual decisions, individual luck, and the interaction of these two, the envy test will no longer be satisfied in respect of the various bundles of resources held. We could constantly redistribute all resources through reruns of the initial auction, but then there would be little satisfaction in planning one's life and little hope of attaining any given ambition. To put the same point another way, there would also be no 'responsibility'. In Dworkin's theory 'responsibility' goes hand in hand

---

[7] Whether the auction device can succeed in this has been doubted, but is not the priority here: see A Halpin, 'Clamshells or Bedsteads?' (2000) 20 *Oxford Journal of Legal Studies* 353–66.

[8] *ER*, n 6 above, p 71.

with not having anyone else run one's life; and with the more 'active' idea of planning for oneself.

Through considering the future from a hypothetically prospective vantage point, Dworkin also draws conclusions about compensation for existing disabilities and disadvantages, including those which are 'accidents of birth'. He does this through use of what he has referred to as the 'insurance principle'.

The 'insurance principle' that Dworkin outlines does commence from the initial auction, or at least from the definition of 'equality' outlined through the medium of the auction device. According to Dworkin's approach to luck, it is not only resources that are chosen (with all that implies about opportunity costs and alternatives foregone) by the participants. Participants will also plan what to do with the bundle of resources that they hold. They may choose to invest those resources in risky but potentially very lucrative ventures, or they may prefer to invest them in safer ventures with more modest rewards. In other words, they will take different risks. According to Dworkin, there is no reason in equality of resources for removing the gains of lucrative risk-taking from those who enjoy 'option luck' of this sort (which stems partly from the decisions about risks which were knowingly taken), in order to enhance the holdings of those who took fewer risks. Equally though, there is no reason to remove gains from the fortunate risk-taker, in order to bail out the person who took the *same* risk, but with different results. Luck, where it is the result of choices, continues to hold in an 'equal' society.

At this point (before considering insurance) we are quite close to outcome responsibility. But the justification offered is not quite the same as the justifications encountered in chapter 4. Dworkin's justification concerns, not the meaning of agency directly, but the question of life-planning in terms of value and preference. Both approaches envisage an 'active individual', but this individual encounters risk in a slightly different way. In Dworkin's case, active individuals must evaluate risks in order to determine which projects are sufficiently valuable to take the chance of an adverse outcome.

The precise reason Dworkin gives for allowing the effects of option luck to stand is slightly suspect, but it may be adapted and made more transparent. He argues that to deny the effects of option luck would be to remove a *choice* from the lives of those concerned. This is not to say that it would 'undo their choice' in the sense that they have followed a particular path and should therefore take the consequences. Once again, the point is about what is 'valued' by individuals, not about holding them to what they actually chose to do. According to Dworkin, both the person who gambled and won, and the person who gambled and lost, chose a life which included risk-taking. If gains and losses were to disappear, both would have removed from them the chance to live a life that includes risks.

In making the point in this way, Dworkin makes his own case a little too easy. He says that risk-taking is something that people want, and illustrates this by the existence of a 'gambling' life style. But while there are many people who enjoy exposure to risk and seek it deliberately for its own sake,[9] many others choose risky ventures not because they positively want to run a risk, but because they are *willing* to do so, in order to attain the potential benefits. I think Dworkin's argument still stands, and if anything the link with insurance works better, if we say instead that to equalise the results of all gambles is unjustified not so much (or not only) because it removes the possibility of a life including risk (risk is desired), but because it removes the *opportunities* associated with risk-taking (risks are seen as worthwhile). I think this works rather better than the justification offered by Dworkin, because it links with his general argument about insurance, that opportunity comes at a cost, and so does security.

If this was Dworkin's last word on the issue of what to do about option luck, then it may well appear to be a rather harsh approach to misfortune, at least where that misfortune is partly self-made. On the other hand, Ripstein has also assumed that Dworkin is over-generous to those who do not 'choose'

[9] A rather smaller subset of these extend enjoyment of risk to key decisions that will determine their future.

(deliberately) to run risks, since he believes Dworkin to suggest that the community has a duty to ensure that brute luck, as opposed to option luck, has no effect whatever on the life of the person concerned. He reads Dworkin as saying that a life should *only* be affected by choices of the individual concerned.[10]

But neither of these is a true reflection of Dworkin's argument. Dworkin uses the device of insurance to moderate both positions, and indeed the precise way that he draws the line between 'brute' and 'option' luck is probably not quite so significant as Ripstein appears to suppose.[11] Instead, the insurance device supplies a method for determining *how much* compensation is payable, and even in cases of 'brute luck' that compensation does not amount to a 'total rescue'. It takes into account the opportunity cost of security.

The Insurance Device

In brief, the insurance device works as follows. If it is appropriate to allow the effects of option luck to stand on grounds of equality, we must also take into account that when people choose to undertake risky enterprises—or even less risky ones—they will often have the opportunity to insure themselves, at least in the ideal conditions of Dworkin's market. Thus insurance—the opportunity to purchase security out of one's bundle of resources—constitutes the link between brute luck and option luck. If we suppose insurance to be available on fair terms,[12] the

[10] A Ripstein, *Equality, Responsibility and the Law* (Cambridge, CUP, 1999) 278–84.

[11] Ripstein does say that he thinks the insurance device 'erases the effects of [Dworkin's] preferred way of drawing the distinction between choices and circumstances' (*ibid,* p 282). Since I read Dworkin as being centrally concerned with answering the questions to which the insurance device applies, and not centrally concerned with distinguishing between brute and option luck for their own sake, the interaction between choice and circumstance in the light of the insurance principle seems to me to be essential.

[12] This is a big assumption–bigger perhaps than Dworkin realises when he describes it as counter-factual. He only discusses the purchase of insurance and its cost according to risk, not the construction of risk-pools essential to the supply of insurance. As explained below, this is important because it ignores the

decision to insure or not to insure means that outcomes flowing from luck of any sort are a question of agency after all.

Because of the supposition of universally available insurance on fair terms, there is now no such thing as 'mere' circumstance in the continuing saga of the desert island immigrants. There are only circumstances in respect of which one has decided to insure or not to insure.[13] Furthermore, risk-taking activities and their consequences can now be tied back to the auction, the envy test, and their respective interpretation of opportunity costs and equality. The premium charged for risk-taking will depend on the opportunity costs of the risk in question. Thus, security will find its appropriate price as the counterpoint to the risk taken. If necessary, people taking large risks will need to settle for a compensation rate that is set rather low—a basic minimum of compensation—and at a high premium. This will be a vital factor when deciding whether to take the risk.

Thus the whole 'choice' about risk-taking is transformed by the presence of insurance. It is not a question of removing risk from the exercise, since all security bears its appropriate price. But it is a question of how much security, at what price, *as well as* how much opportunity, at what risk, the decision-maker prefers.

Up to this point, I think the operation of the insurance device is consistent with the envy test stated in a modified way, although Dworkin does not say so explicitly. We could imagine a point in time at which the resource-holders decide what to do with the resources they hold, what risks to take and what opportunities to pursue. By taking such a hypothetically prospective vantage point, we should in principle see that each person actually prefers their life plan—and the whole bundle of resources and risks/ opportunities they select—to the life plan of others. Each person should feel comfortable that they are taking the risks and pursuing the opportunities that they prefer, while

sources and conditions of shared security. But supply-side issues are also relevant to the issue of pricing.

[13] This assumes the foreseeability of various relevant hazards.

insuring to some optimal level (bearing in mind the costs) against the worst outcomes. We can tell that luck has now entered the frame, however, because those participants will not necessarily think that their life-plan was best when they look back on it. There are no grounds for constant reruns of our life choices on the basis of *regret*, in the way that we reran the auction on the basis of envy.

This last point is significant, because its effect is carried over into the operation of the insurance principle in conditions of *unequal antecedent circumstances*, as opposed to different luck over time. Here, Dworkin takes a further single step towards reality, and away from the assumptions of the desert island. He considers how we should respond to inequalities which are not based wholly on luck as it affects future plans, but which are heavily influenced by existing circumstances. This is a key transition in his argument, because for the most part people do not face equal antecedent risks and opportunities. They do not have the same skills, tastes, or predispositions; they do not command equal resources on any definition; and they may face genetic predisposition to handicap or suffer from congenital disability. We have therefore arrived at the central question. *Given* unequal antecedent circumstances, what transfer from fortunate to unfortunate is justified in the name of equality?

Dworkin's answer is *not* that we should choose the transfer that will undo brute luck; nor is it that we should choose the transfer that will satisfy the envy test at any given time.[14] Instead, the transfer which Dworkin proposes as justified by the insurance principle is modelled on the insurance cover that *would have been chosen* by people if they could have contemplated the relevant risk from a (counter-factual) position of equal exposure to that risk.

---

[14] He is explicit about both of these. As to the first, see R Dworkin, 'Justice, Insurance and Luck' in *Sovereign Virtue*, (Cambridge, MA, Harvard University Press, 2000) 320, 341 (hereinafter '*JIL*'). As to the second, see *ER*, n 6 above, p 104: in a society operating the insurance principle, 'some people have much more than others of what both desire, through no reason connected with choice'.

Here, we are treating the envy test as no longer decisive because it is in these circumstances *akin to regret* and, as we saw above, regret is not a reason to rerun our choices. When we make choices under uncertainty, we know that we may win or lose. The point of insurance decisions is to make both of these possibilities at least tolerable, and hopefully to hold them in balance. If we 'win' the insurance bet, and actually do need to claim on the policy that we choose,[15] then we will not have everything from life that we hoped for. That is inherent in the idea that security comes at a price, and that we would not give up all opportunities just in order to secure a possible advantage should we turn out to be less talented or able bodied than others.

Dworkin explains that no-one, from a hypothetical position of ignorance about risks, would make the sort of insurance decision that would provide enough compensation to satisfy the envy test at any given moment. For example, we would not choose a policy that would grant us movie star earnings should we turn out to lack talent, looks and application sufficient to earn those sums in reality. That policy would be far too costly, and if we 'lost' the insurance bet (ie, if we turned out to possess the requisite talent, looks, and application), we would effectively be enslaved to a life of money-making just in order to pay the premium. Similarly, in the case of medical intervention, we would not 'choose' an expensive insurance premium which would cover a total rescue plan and perhaps speculative medical intervention, because this would tie us to a very high premium should we 'lose' the insurance bet and remain healthy. Thus, it would not be justified for a government to fund such a plan, either.[16] By the same token however, governments *are* justified in imposing a tax and transfer scheme to the level that *would* supposedly be chosen by those ignorant of their specific risks, in the case of those risks (which I have suggested above is most of them) which are not equally shared.

[15] Which is to say, if we are losers in other respects.
[16] *JIL*, n 14 above, p 343.

It is implicit in all of this, of course, that we can specify what insurance people would have bought, had they experienced equality in their exposure to risk. Dworkin assumes that we can do this on the basis of 'average' preference curves. He probably further assumes that there will be considerable grouping around the mean. Thus, he treats reactions to risk as variable, but only within certain limits; and he further assumes (guided by economic theory) that there is a broad level of predictability in the purchasing decisions that would be reached by rational consumers of insurance. Not only does this depend on the existence of some significant regularity in the response to risks and opportunities, it also holds people to an average, and treats that average as providing an insight into that which is just and equal.

Issues and Implications

The 'insurance principle' explained above allows Dworkin to make some important and distinctive claims. First, he is able to argue that there are some reasons based in equality and fairness for saying that there is an entitlement to a certain level of welfare provision in respect of each aspect of inequality, apparently going beyond a basic minimum, and therefore a responsibility on those who enjoy net good luck (for the time being) to contribute through taxation. At the same time, he offers a reason why those who are claiming support may be told that a limited level of compensation (and not a total rescue) is also fair. This has nothing to do with 'levelling down', and everything to do with opportunity costs. Second, these arguments appear to be based in ideas of agency, responsibility and choice, not in charity or the claim that those in need deserve to be helped purely in virtue of their need.

Both of these apparent features could be said to be illusory to some extent, or at least to be more limited than appears at first sight. I will deal first with the second point (agency, responsibility and choice), and will return to the appropriate level and coverage of welfare provision after that.

Responsibility and choice are components of the *hypothetical* insurance system, in which people would choose the level at which they wished to insure, on the basis of a level playing field. But where the provision of *actual* welfare support is concerned, payments must necessarily be decided without reference to the real choices of the individual recipient, or the choices of anyone else. Only hypothetical choices are available. Although Dworkin emphasises not only subjectivity but also variety in the value that will be attached both to resources and to risk-taking, there is said to be sufficient uniformity in the 'preference curves' of individuals in general, to conclude what the average hypothetical choice of security and risk will be. To the extent that he persuades us that this has any universal implications for justice and equality, Dworkin does so by concentrating mainly on the likely *cost* of insurance, giving a sense of 'objectivity' in the examination of which type of insurance is likely to be worthwhile, or not worthwhile. In other words, Dworkin exploits the apparently technical and 'objective' features of risk, in the form of actuarial calculation, and at this point seems to underplay subjective elements which were so crucial to earlier parts of his theory.

The extent to which Dworkin's approach truly depends on responsibility is this. Ultimately, he contends that there is a degree of inequality which we must accept, because if we were planning responsibly for the risks of life from a fair starting point, we would see that the opportunity costs of making good all inequalities would be too great. However, it is only because of the prospective form of insurance that it appears to make this a matter of calculation *within the individual's life*. When we cease to look at prospective risks, and look instead at existing misfortunes and inequalities *as if* in a prospective way, then we are in fact saying that the opportunity cost *to others* is too great to provide more than a particular level of support. In part, this is deployed as a way of urging those who suffer misfortune to accept a limit to their claim for support: they are asked to examine, hypothetically, what opportunities they would have given up in advance, to achieve the kind of security, income or assistance that would be implied. But it is also, more clearly, a basis for arguing that the unfortunate are not making an unreasonable claim when they seek an appropriate level of support.

Despite Dworkin's apparent assertion that certain risks must be shouldered and dealt with by individuals, the argument for limited support is nevertheless importantly different from both neo-liberalism and 'third way' theories, which propose that individuals must, even given unequal and uncertain conditions, indeed choose for themselves. Both of these approaches emphasise self-sufficiency in the handling of risks, with more (according to the third way) or less (according to the neo-liberals) supporting intervention. Dworkin emphasises the responsibility for planning one's life, but with particular emphasis on the basic values and aspirations of a life, not on the actual processes by which the right level of security is negotiated. In this respect, his 'individualism' remains very different from the 'individualisation' described by Elisabeth Beck-Gernsheim, for example, and further explored below.[17] Dworkin's individuals are 'sovereign', but not necessarily self-sufficient.

Our other significant question concerned the level and extent of support that is justified by the theory, and to whom it is available. Here, Dworkin seeks to mark out a contrast with Rawls' 'maximin' solution, by which participants choose the solution with the 'least worst' outcome. Instead, he says that his insurance principle can apply to each and every individual, rather than simply to a 'class' defined as the least well-off. Importantly, this enables Dworkin to present welfare as a common concern, based on security, rather than a marginal concern, based on need. There is an inclusiveness in Dworkin's approach which certainly reflects its origins in insurance. When put into practice, Rawls' theory by contrast attends only (in terms of distribution of material goods) to the needs of the least well off. As is well known, Rawls comes to this conclusion by applying contentious

[17] E Beck-Gernsheim, M Chalmers (tr), 'Life as a Planning Project', in S Lash, B Szerszynski and B Wynne (eds), *Risk, Environment and Modernity: Towards a New Ecology* (London, Sage, 1996). For Beck-Gernsheim, in 'individualised' society the emphasis is on being well-informed about risk and security options, and learning to treat oneself (quoting from U Beck's *Risk Society* (London, Sage, 1992) 135) as a 'planning office' with respect to one's own biography (p 140).

assumptions about common responses to risks.[18] As Dworkin comments, this does not provide any protection against insecurity for those who are just above this level, nor for people in general.[19]

The lack of inclusiveness in Rawls' theory is significant. The theory has been treated, by Peter Baldwin, as providing a liberal-philosophical route to solidarity. Baldwin argues that through Rawls' method, 'common vulnerability fosters solidarity', making it a hypothetical/ philosophical version of social insurance systems.[20] But Rawls' theory places all its arguments about shared uncertainty at a deeply hypothetical stage, and at no point underlines that the sharing of uncertainty is a part of the real-life solution to insecurity and thus inequality. Furthermore, the outcome of the very abstract and hypothetical shared vulnerability created by Rawls in the original position is a

[18] Pertinently, it has been asked why Rawls thinks the participants in the original position would necessarily choose to adopt a maximin solution, rather than a (slightly more daring) insurance strategy: RM Hare, 'Rawls' Theory of Justice' in N Daniels (ed), *Reading Rawls* (New York, NY, Basic Books, 1975). The insurance strategy, he suggests, would set only a minimum of assured protection, in the same way that people insure against calamity but then are prepared to take risks provided some basic cover is obtained. Once this minimum level is attained, Hare suggests there will be no reason to continue preferring the least well-off group, or (in the conditions of the original position) to continue ensuring that the least good outcome is as good as possible. Risky opportunities, he thinks, may well be preferred. Though sharing something with Dworkin in terms of method, this is in a sense the opposite conclusion from that reached by Dworkin, since it suggests that to think in terms of insurance will tend to lead to a more minimal level of concern for the least well off than that proposed by Rawls. But one reason for this is that Hare starts from the original position in order to test Rawls' conclusions, whereas Dworkin does not. Another is that Dworkin takes more seriously the felt need to secure at least a proportion of what one has or of what is on offer, rather than just a basic minimum. Thus he is concerned with security, rather than a basic safety net. Hare's conclusions may give us further reasons for saying that the abstract argument about decision-making under uncertainty to be found in Rawls' *Theory of Justice* is a less potent way of getting social welfare to be accepted, than the felt need for security which lies behind social insurance schemes.

[19] *ER*, n 6 above, pp 113–17.

[20] Baldwin, n 2 above, p 34.

recommendation not of security for all, but of limited redistribution only to that group who lose out the most.[21] This is not equivalent to 'universality' in Baldwin's sense.

Does Dworkin come closer to providing a liberal route to solidarity? Dworkin contrasts with Rawls in arguing that in order to assess the appropriate level of security for each of us, it will be important to decide on the basis of a more informed self-interest what compromises we are willing to make. The self-interest in question takes account of our life plans and priorities; but knowledge is still limited because we are not aware of other factors which would affect our particular vulnerability. As already mentioned, this makes security a common, not a marginal concern. However, Dworkin still does not fully catch onto the solidaristic aspect of insurance. He discusses insurance in terms of opportunity costs and compromise between security and opportunity. He does not discuss the degree to which, through insurance, the shared uncertainty of each contributes to the security of all, through the pooling of risk. Dworkin's insurance is concerned with compromise, pricing and the decision to purchase; *not* in the end with the sources of security and the building of risk pools. Yet it is in the very construction of such sources of security that we will find the key to 'solidarity'.

Perhaps the key difference between Dworkin's theory, and those social policy regimes which are actually constructed upon insurance, is that the social insurance systems are theorised as being constructed on a 'political' settlement or factual (not hypothetical) social contract. Thus there is a popular connection with the technique of insurance, as a collective resource. Dworkin uses the *device* of insurance, but he does so on the basis of individual personal choices and without reference to the politics of solidarity. His approach appeals to market competition and the *pricing* of one's choices relative to others, rather than the idea that we stand together and even, through contributions, each provide the others' security. The key advantage of

---

[21] It should be clear that this attends only to the material aspect of Rawls' theory, rather than to the distribution of liberties and rights.

Dworkin's approach is that it enables reflection on the meaning of equality. Its key disadvantage is that it misses out on the strongest historical lessons of what might be achieved via the interdependence involved in risk pooling. Dworkin's approach is not in the end as topical as he proposes. Insurance is a thought experiment, not a mechanism, on his approach. He does not after all show how to adapt insurance approaches to meet new circumstances, and especially changing ideas of responsibility.

In summary, Dworkin is clear that the extent to which the community as a whole is responsible for 'rescuing' those in trouble is limited and that this is consistent with personal responsibility, including the idea of responsibility for planning one's life. His social vision differs from that of social insurance in the continental European mode,[22] because apart from the existence of limited community responsibility, there is no express mention of solidarity or social contract. The contractual analogies we may draw with Dworkin's theory are less explicitly political, being concerned instead with the rational decisions of individuals seeking to 'maximise their preferences' over a life. Dworkin's interdependence is the interdependence of opportunity costs, rather than of mutually provided security. Despite the insurance 'model', the form of delivery of benefits is likely to be payments funded from taxation, not insurance derived from premiums or contributions.

On the other hand, Dworkin differs decidedly from neo-liberals, in that he does not suggest that 'responsibility' is an idea at odds with the welfare state, nor that the best way to eradicate poverty is to abolish welfare and end dependency. Neither is his

---

[22] 'Continental' social insurance systems are most centrally associated with those systems modelled on or resembling the German model of social insurance. They include not only the German but also the French and Italian systems. It is generally accepted that the British and Scandinavian welfare states were initially constructed upon more egalitarian principles than the core 'continental' systems: see for example G Esping-Andersen, 'Welfare States Without Work: the Impasse of Labour Shedding and Familialism in Continental European Social Policy' in G Esping-Andersen (ed), *Welfare States in Transition* (London, Sage, 1996).

insurance schema the same as the 'third way', despite a passing resemblance and a shared interest in the insurance technique. In particular, he does not give individuals the heavy responsibility of becoming expert risk assessors adept at finding their way through the jungle of contemporary risks and available forms of security. Individuals are perceived as holding the responsibility for planning a life, setting priorities, and determining what is 'valuable' and to be preferred, although it seems we are able to 'second guess' many aspects of these tasks where security and opportunity costs are in question. Individuals do not need to run a virtual 'planning office' for their own biography,[23] determine what is on offer, and opt for the best products available for the achievement of their security.

Dworkin borrows certain aspects of real insurance, most notably its prospectivity, to transform the relevant questions and seek a welcome escape from entrenched positions. But his insurance remains hypothetical, a device of imagination aimed, rather like Rawls' veil of ignorance, at getting people to see beyond self-interested positions of knowing advantage and privileged self-reliance in security planning. It goes so far as to imagine a shared need for security, while Rawls asked us to imagine how we would distribute scarce resources to the least well off. But it does not propose that such a shared need really exists, nor explore the way that the existence of such a shared need is the very occasion and opportunity for its resolution.

2. Mutuality and Solidarity

It will be remembered that Ewald's analysis of risk (explored in chapter 2 above) included an argument that the key structures of insurance society are not individualistic but *collective*. The key to such societies is not so much responsibility, which he associated with the preceding liberal and *juridical* regime, but *solidarity*. The paradigm of responsibility gave way to the paradigm of solidarity.

[23] Beck-Gernsheim, n 17 above.

On my analysis immediately above, this idea of 'solidarity' is not matched by anything in liberal theory. Dworkin, for example, might be said to provide reasons for acting with respect for others, or for computing the 'costs' of one's choices in terms of opportunity costs to oneself or others. But there, 'others' are people whose interests and plans compete with one's own, and the point is to compete fairly. The idea of solidarity based on the practice of insurance implies instead that there is a different sort of interdependence between people. It is true that society itself exposes me to certain risks; but other people, and our reciprocal burden of risk, are also the source of my security. I suggested that to overlook the *construction* of common risk pools led Dworkin to ignore supply-side issues, undermining his argument from pricing; but that his argument was also therefore less politically engaged than he had hoped. Now it is time to question the idea of solidarity a little.

It is important to notice that the kind of interdependence encountered in social insurance is made possible by the prospective vantage point through which risk is assessed, and by the continuation of uncertainty[24] of a type which renders each individual 'subject to' the risk. On Ewald's account, 'solidarity' is not so much a driving force or sentiment which brings about insurance society. Rather, it is an effect or implication of the new technology of insurance, since this technology acts to pool risks and therefore to solidify interests.

But it is also important that the contours of the insurance society are defined through negotiation and social contract. Some researchers have explained the enduring support for continental social insurance systems in terms of the long-standing settlements between different influential groups that they represent—particularly in the traditional employment sectors. Political support, once built, may continue long after the initial

---

[24] This is not 'uncertainty' in the technical sense of being incapable of calculation. Rather, this is a form of uncertainty which makes it possible to approach individuals' probability of accident as roughly comparable, even when not equal; and which does not allow it to be said which individuals are 'free' from particular risks or 'certain' to contract a particular loss.

mutuality of interest has faded. Interestingly, it is also observed that these structures are, as a result, rather conservative, and that they have begun to deal badly with the changing needs of contemporary economies. They are based as much on historical accident concerning the needs of particular interest groups, as on the evolution of new techniques. Worse, they are accused of creating 'insiders' and 'outsiders' (the latter including those who have never been in traditional, secure employment; and also many women), at a time when the welfare state is in need of more contributing individuals.[25] Many commentators have now begun to observe that the preferred solution is not so much to be found in revisions to the social contract, as in the evolution of a new era of individualisation, and of personal responsibility.

Individuals and Responsibility in 'Insurance Society'

Given this new emphasis on 'individualisation', it is important to remind ourselves of one or two observations concerning *individuals* in 'insurance society'. First, Ewald suggested that the structures of insurance society largely left the individual untouched, demanding far less of his or her allegiance than earlier forms of solidarity such as the family, religion, or trade unions. This was the mirror-image of Simon's argument that 'actuarial' methods provide more effective forms of regulation partly because they make little or no appeal in terms felt or understood by the populace—they seem universal, removed, professional. Simon argued that risk society overlooks the individual; Ewald suggested that insurance leaves the individual free. But both interpretations now encounter a further important possibility: that individuals are increasingly required to think and to plan in the same 'risk management' terms on their own account. In other words, risk technology *cannot* leave the individual free.

---

[25] Primarily, this is because of an ageing population and (with greater life expectancy) a greater retirement period. Also implicated though are low fertility rates in European countries, and the mixed success of inclusion of women in the workforce. Esping-Andersen, n 22 above, convincingly relates these latter problems to lack of child-care provision and ungenerous maternity rights and pay in certain of the continental systems.

The ubiquitous actuarial logic touches lives, too. Thus while Beck presents 'risk society' as including at some level an opportunity to obtain release from the institutional methods of industrial society, it is possible that uncertainty and individualisation will simply enhance the obligation of all citizens to reason in this way, but this time on their own account.

Further, Ewald observed that responsibility certainly does not disappear in the society newly dominated by insurance. Rather, responsibility is transformed. Whereas historically, it was thought inappropriate to permit insurance against liability for events that were one's fault, with the transformation to insurance society 'to be responsible' (or to act responsibly) is precisely *to be insured.* In some respects, this gives rise to extra social obligations. Not to carry insurance is to breach a social obligation, whether this is the obligation to provide cover to others, or to cover one's own potential losses.[26]

But more contemporaneous shifts being identified in the nature and social importance of 'risk' may have far-reaching effects for a society which is increasingly widely conceded to have become, to some degree, *'assurancielle'* (dominated by insurance). In brief, these include a greater institutional tolerance of risk; and (associated with this), greater emphasis on the individual to do more than to hold insurance where it is recommended or required. The individual now has a key role in risk planning and in managing the future. The individual's 'obligations' include not just 'doing the responsible thing' (compliance with obligations, or choosing security, in the form of insurance), but *being self-reliant.* This leads us to consider whether a new kind of focus on the individual is emerging.

[26] F Ewald, 'Genetics, Insurance and Risk' in T McGleenan, U Wiesing and F Ewald (eds), *Genetics and Insurance,* (Oxford, BIOS Scientific Publishers, 1999).

3. Beyond Solidarity?—Individualisation, Differentiation, and Responsibility

There are a number of contexts in which responsibility has become newly dominant as an idea in connection with risk. Yet this does not take us back to an old fashioned culpability notion, nor to the liberal updatings of responsibility encountered in chapter 4 and in this chapter. The new kind of focus upon the individual takes a very risk-conscious form. Indeed, the whole *nature* of what it means to focus on the individual appears to be changing.

Individualisation

There are at least three strands to the idea of 'individualisation' as it is currently discussed. The first of these has already been mentioned: the increasing emphasis on individuals to carry out the role of life-planner on their own account, and especially to act as negotiator of risks and consumer of security. This tends to draw us back from a sense of interdependence, to an idea of self-sufficiency in the planning of security. An idea of self-sufficiency among the best-off was, according to Baldwin, a precursor to the development of 'universal' or solidaristic social welfare systems. Only when many of those who had previously felt self-sufficient realised the extent of their own exposure to risk was social insurance rendered universal. By contrast, the new emphasis on self-sufficiency seems to come at a time when the increasing *in*security of working arrangements in particular is also apparent.[27]

The second strand concerns absence of institutional restraints on our lives. Both Beck and Giddens discuss this in terms of 'post-traditionalism', and emphasise the new responsibilities and opportunities that this brings for *planning one's own biography*.

[27] Beck refers to a new preponderance of short-term, 'flexible' working, and little or no long-term security or pension rights for employees: E Beck, P Camiller (tr), *The Brave New World of Work* (Cambridge, Polity Press, 2000) ch 1.

This is meant to relate to our plans and styles of life in general, and not just to questions of material security and exposure to risk. But this can, again, be linked to risk and insecurity in a different form. Bauman explains that our forebears thought of freedom in terms of lack of control, or not being told what to do: 'by that definition, they would probably describe the situation most of us are in today as freedom incarnate'. But that freedom, for Bauman, comes at the heavy price of 'insecurity'. No one seems to be in control, and 'it is the acting person who is bound to pay the costs of the risks taken'.[28] Absence of constraint itself enhances risks, and also enhances responsibility.

That observation leads us to the third strand in individualisation—the absence of a set frame of reference within which we might reach our decisions, and make those decisions with confidence. Bauman in particular has emphasised that this phenomenon—this awareness of change and of the provisional nature of all judgments and predictions—has a disabling effect on the thoughts and actions of individuals in general. This tends to be an overlooked aspect of the processes by which risk decisions are, in recognition of their subjectivity and the specifics of each case, increasingly entrusted to individuals. Bauman proposes that those individuals are in turn unable to make confident use of the methods of decision-making, because of awareness of the very factors (generally, flaws in the method) which have led them to be entrusted to the individual level. This recognition, combined with underestimation of its effects, are important background to the discussion of collective decision-making, and the development of precaution, in chapter 6.

Increasing differentiation and discrimination in insurance practice?

Of course, discrimination has always been an essential tool of insurance. This is part of the whole 'technology of risk'—to ascribe risk features in terms of probability to a *class*.

[28] Z Bauman, *The Individualized Society* (Cambridge, Polity Press, 2001) 44–45.

Differentiation between classes is as central as creation of classes. As such, the relationship between insurance and justice is bound to be problematic at some level. Ewald has glossed over this problem, arguing that 'mutuality' insurance is conducive to the significant transition to solidarity described above. It is the insurance mechanism itself which matters. This is part of his point: to stress the continuities between continental social insurance systems and other systems including market-led insurance. Baldwin however emphasises that only when risk pools are generalised can there be said to be solidarity: he defines solidarity *in terms of* universality. And other commentators have argued that there is a clear and very significant difference between two basic types of insurance.

For example, O'Neill explains that 'mutuality' insurance is premised on the idea that a fair premium is paid according to differential risks.[29] The underlying principle of fairness is represented in the idea of 'utmost good faith': no party should try to conceal the extent of the risk they pose. Discrimination, of relevant types, is therefore central to mutuality insurance. 'Solidarity-based' insurance systems, she argues, are more egalitarian. Insurance based on 'solidarity' does not discriminate between individuals on the basis of their different risks; instead, it offers universal coverage and tends to require near-universal contribution. Those with least risk often pay more than those with greater risk, since contributions are often linked to income, and many (though not all) risks are *inverse* to income.

It is relatively easy to see how systems which appear to work on the basis of contributions—'social insurance' systems of the continental type—might be able to maintain greater support for longer than out and out 'needs-benefits' systems, as traditionally seen in the UK. The appearance of matching entitlements to contributions is often misleading, but there is generally a perception that people in such systems actually 'stand together' as the members of risk pools are intended to do in the case of

[29] O O'Neill, 'Insurance and Genetics: The Current State of Play' (1998) 61 *Modern Law Review* 716–23.

mutuality insurance. The continental social insurance systems have therefore borrowed some of the advantages of mutuality insurance. The evolution of solidarity in such systems might be considered to have two stages. First, socialised insurance provides the very idea of mutual support; second, insurance is extended beyond broad identity of risks. Though these extensions may be controversial and dependent on political factors and a contingent coincidence of interests,[30] the principle that what is being supplied is security rather than, say, charitable assistance tends to remain intact even though protection is broadened beyond the common risk pool.

O'Neill herself does not seek to explain the *sources* of solidarity however. As explained above, the French and German social security arrangements as a whole were not in their origins predominantly aimed at egalitarianism, but at income maintenance, above all for those in employment. They can be interpreted as remaining highly conservative, and unprogressive.[31]

For Ewald's purposes, perhaps the distinction between mutuality and solidarity-based insurance seemed hardly to matter, since the historic rise of insurance to cover the primary societal risks—to health, to employment, and from accidents, for example—had major effects whether based on mutuality principles or not. But in contemporary conditions, the basis of insurance and the extent to which it is compatible with social justice become particularly important and connected questions.

The two examples explored below consider changing conditions in two different ways. The first concerns changes in the potential methods for dividing risks and assessing susceptibility of individuals or groups; the second concerns changes in the methods and market philosophy of insurance.

(a) Genetic Testing and Insurance

A major set of challenges for insurance is posed by the growth of genetic testing. Increasingly, it is becoming possible to test for

[30] This is essentially Badwin's thesis: see n 2 above.

[31] Esping-Andersen, 'Welfare States Without Work', n 22 above.

the presence of genetic markers which will increase, decrease, or exclude the risk of certain inherited conditions. Here, the fear has arisen that insurers may be able to gain access to information which would enable risk differentiation of a new sort.[32] For one thing, the risks in question would be fundamental to the individuals concerned and indeed physically inseparable from them. There is nothing that the risk-carrier can do to avoid the risk. On some level, genetic discrimination therefore appears comparable to race discrimination. To this, the insurers' riposte is that whereas race discrimination is unjustified on a mutuality basis,[33] there is every reason (within a mutuality framework) for excluding bad risks, and therefore for excluding those with particularly enhanced genetic risks. Any other solution would be unfair to 'low risk' customers. Genetic discrimination is therefore not 'arbitrary'. The question arises of whether there are reasons of *justice* for protecting people *from* the kind of 'fairness' seen in mutuality insurance.

Another reason why the new information on genetic predisposition poses fresh challenges is that in some cases it seems to provide a form of information which is much more potent than the usual 'risk information'. Most risk information is statistical— one must be content with being ranked as 'high risk' or as 'normal'. Occasionally, one may be 'low risk'. Certain of the new genetic tests can provide the information that a specific individual will not develop a particular condition, or that another individual will—given enough years of life—be likely to develop the same condition. Thus, populations can be more decisively divided at the individual level, and it is no longer a case of small variations between individuals in the terms on which insurance is offered.

[32] British insurers have tended to suggest that this kind of information is in fact no different from any other used in underwriting.

[33] Arguably, it is an indication of the weakness of mutuality as a principle of fairness that there may well be actuarial reasons for discrimination on the basis of race (or gender, sexual orientation, or social class). The very existence of discrimination at large leaves excluded groups more open to certain risks.

Ewald has recently questioned the significance of such developments, and this questioning gives us an insight into the nature of the 'solidarity' he describes.[34] He uses at least three arguments to defend the stance of insurers, who have argued that genetic information should be at their disposal.[35] One is simply that they are acting fairly, in that 'mutuality' depends on the attribution of relevant risk scores. This tends to underline the contingent nature of Ewald's solidarity, resting as it does on factors such as relevant uncertainty, shared exposure, and sufficiently large risk pools. Again this is consistent with the dominance of technology in bringing about forms of governance. Being essentially an *effect* of these factors, solidarity can hardly be a principle *opposed to* mutuality. We have already questioned this, and observed that the link between mutuality and solidarity is now fragile.

Ewald's response is particularly hard-line. One might have thought that the over all growth of a politics of solidarity, which he also describes, could have been deployed to explain the general public sentiment—at least so far—against the use of genetic information by insurers. To date, as Husted observes, it has *not* been the reaction of most people with 'normal' genetic risks that those at higher risk should be excluded from the common pool.[36] This raises the possibility that we might *choose* solidarity, for whatever reason,[37] where mutuality runs out. I think Ewald here understates the extent to which some social insurance systems have depended on extension of solidarity principles well beyond mutuality, and in some respects in a fashion which is directly inverse to mutuality.

[34] Ewald, n 26 above.

[35] This issue has been resolved at least temporarily in many countries through voluntary agreement of insurers. In the UK, following protracted enquiry, argument and negotiation, the insurers have agreed to a 5 year moratorium on use of genetic information in underwriting.

[36] J Husted, 'Insurance, Genetics and Solidarity' in McGleenan, Wiesing and Ewald (eds), *Genetics and Insurance,* (Oxford, BIOS Scientific Publishers, 1999).

[37] For example on the basis of arguments about equality, like Dworkin's, or because we have become accustomed to it through the experience of social insurance.

Ewald's second argument against the use of genetic information is that there is no reason for 'socialising' life insurance in the way that health care, in particular, has been socialised. This latter argument is puzzling, given Ewald's own account of the ubiquity of insurance and its centrality in delivering security in modern societies. Here, it might be argued, the issue is one of *exclusion*. Though Ewald here chooses to perceive life insurance narrowly as securing a sum of money should one die, to be left by way of inheritance, life assurance is also vital in the UK market (for example) for the offer of a mortgage. The narrower view overlooks the dimension of a *need to be secured* through insurance, before one can participate in such a key process as property ownership. Ewald goes further, suggesting that 'average risk' consumers would be likely to quit insurance altogether, if they felt that insurance was being used as a means of 'stimulating spending'. Apart from ignoring the effects of uninsurability in respect of life cover, this also implies that people *would* think it unfair for those at high risk to be offered cover, and also overlooks the fact that most consumers *could not afford* to do without life insurance, because it is a condition of borrowing. In other words, what Ewald does is to try to protect the 'purity' of mutuality and the rights of the insurers to act in a commercially viable way. He does this by denying both the social importance of the broad forms of security provided through insurance, and the democratic sentiment that the practice of insurance brings.

The third argument is that insurers have not been the driving force behind the acquisition of new information in respect of genetic risks, and that their thirst for such knowledge is exaggerated. According to Ewald, insurers need only the *efficient minimum* of information to make their decisions: they need to acquire 'a minimum of useful information'. If genetic information introduces too many variables, then the information will become difficult to exploit. Ewald here is encouraging the view that what insurers need is relative simplicity in information, allowing the most profitable division of risks. The implication is that insurers only need to use the information provided by genetic testing to the extent that its usefulness outweighs the

148

associated costs, and that this is likely to limit the extent of any such use.

Is this last argument simply a wilful attempt to keep mutuality and solidarity in tune? Here the *details* of insurance systems seem genuinely all-important. In the UK, 65 insurance companies admitted receiving genetic test information, and using it in a number of cases, before the voluntary agreement reached in 2001. On the other hand, it could be that many insurers are in truth relieved to be able to offer insurance without taking into account a further form of information, provided they can be assured that other companies are playing by the same rules, and provided that issues of adverse selection are dealt with.[38] After all, information is costly to process.

Debates over use of genetic test results have been had, with broadly the same conclusions, in many jurisdictions, variation centring mainly on whether the bar on use of these results takes the form of voluntary agreement or of legislation, and whether it is temporary or permanent in form. Genetic testing is a particular issue where an egalitarian spirit, whether liberal or solidarity-based, has so far proved resistant to pressure for greater differentiation for particular reasons. For example, Husted may be right in thinking that for many people, the results of medical research should not be used outside the medical context.

The issue of genetic testing is a relatively discrete one, albeit symptomatic of wider concerns, in which legislation can indeed be used to prevent the drift towards greater differentiation and demarcation, and where such legislation can even deal with the primary concerns of insurers.[39] It is also an issue where the at-risk group have not so far been 'demonised' in the way that

[38] 'Adverse selection' in this instance is the phenomenon whereby those who know they are likely to be incapacitated or die early buy disproportionately high levels of insurance in order to safeguard their own or their dependents' interests, thus distorting the risk pool.

[39] The existing arrangement deals with adverse selection simply by setting a cap on the insured amount to which genetic test information will be disregarded.

welfare claimants (for example) often are.[40] But apart from the specific issue of genetic testing, there is also new work suggesting that insurers do in fact demand the creation and dissemination of information of increasing sophistication. This is not so much because of changes in availability of information, but because of changing market philosophies relevant to insurance.

(b) Differentiation and division?

According to Ericson, Barry and Doyle,[41] processes of differentiation and division, of breaking down or segmenting the risk pool rather than of pooling risks, now begin to dominate the insurance industry.[42] Clearly, any such trend toward differentiation or 'unpooling' would work to the short-term benefit of those who are 'low risk',[43] but may result in hefty premiums, or even exclude altogether, those who are considered 'high risk'. Furthermore, treatment of the 'high risk' can be rough indeed, with specialist firms springing up specifically to cover 'high risks' at special rates—and employing not their own claims managers, but hired guns to check for wrongdoing among those making claims. These firms exploit the compulsory nature of insurance, but their approach succeeds in encouraging more 'high risk' individuals to avoid taking out insurance at all.

The net effect is to dilute the 'socializing' influence of insurance. Ericson et al regard this as being, in part, a response to global competitive pressures. New institutions have entered the insurance market, which have carved out their own niche in

[40] Having said this, it is important not to be over-optimistic. For example, there are already signs that those with genetic susceptibilities are regarded at least among some experts as to be praised for deciding not to have genetic offspring. See E Beck-Gernsheim, 'Life as a Planning Project', n 17 above, pp 147–48.

[41] R Ericson, D Barry and A Doyle, 'The Moral Hazards of Neo-Liberalism: Lessons From the Private Insurance Industry' (2000) 4 *Economy and Society* 532–58.

[42] Their research was carried out in Canada. They suggest that the same process is more advanced in the United States, where neo-liberal politics are more deeply entrenched.

[43] There is not necessarily any group of consumers who will benefit from this trend in the long term.

covering 'preferred' clients; other new institutions enter to deal with those now excluded. Thus, the authors conclude that these developments can be linked to neo-liberalism in that they stem from the same pressures which have given rise to the general growth of neo-liberal philosophy. Much more loosely though, it might be concluded from the account of Ericson et al that the dominance of neo-liberalism in political terms nurtures the practices in question, through encouraging an atmosphere of self-reliance and discouraging regulatory demands against too much segmentation or de-selection. For example, they outline the way that employment practices within the insurance industry mirror the fragmentation of the product, as sales are made and claims dealt with by an increasingly agency-based and insecure, short-term work force. This is one indication that insurance is in turn part of the insecure (or in neo-liberal terms, 'dynamic') economic sector, no longer predominantly a professionalised service industry.

There is some further evidence in the research presented by Ericson et al that the security actually provided by insurance is changing. At its extreme, where accident insurance was concerned, one industry insider commented that the product could now hardly be called 'insurance' at all. Even a single claim in some sectors could cause the claimant to be recategorised as 'high risk', whereas in the past an unusually bad claims history in a short space of time was required. This partly reflects a pre-occupation with 'moral hazard' and the perceived need to avoid fraudulent claims. But the findings are suggestive of a greater change, through which insurance begins to resemble something like outcome responsibility. This is however a very different kind of outcome responsibility from that painstakingly justified by liberal legal writers. It makes no reference to agency, being a development of actuarial science but in a 'disaggregated' form. Potentially, it is the mere fact of having made a claim that can place the individual in a new category. The interpretation of an accident as a unique occurrence, as opposed to the statistical exposure to risk of an expected kind, is back; but this time without an emphasis on 'ill-will', or indeed any exercise of will at all.

The consignment to insurance on 'special terms' is the new liability.

Ericson et al further argue that the insurance market in neo-liberal political conditions operates with considerable emphasis on policing of fraud and on 'moral hazard'. Thus it is a market in which the typical 'state' strategies of surveillance, management and policing of fraud are deployed instead by private actuarial organizations. Thus they describe this scenario in terms of the 'governance of institutionalised individualism'. In these conditions of institutionalised individualism, they argue, people are *required* to exercise *choice* and *agency*; they do **not** experience *freedom* or *liberty*. We could say, building on the discussion in this and earlier chapters, that such individuals may be 'active', but nevertheless compelled to be active in a particular way. They are compelled to act as part of 'risk society', and not only to comply with its safety rituals,[44] but also to seek out the right products to protect their security.

If Ewald is correct about historical developments, then there was a time when to act responsibly was to carry insurance. Now, responsibility is considerably more demanding of individuals. Individuals must be self-sufficient; if they are unable to gain insurance from one source, they must cover their risks and 'bounce back' some other way. This touches deeper themes about the nature of individualised society, and especially the insecurity and isolation of the 'choosing individual' in such circumstances.

For lawyers, the nature of responsibility and its relationship with rights is an issue of persisting interest. For Dworkin, rights and responsibilities are simply two sides of the same coin, to the extent that the one can even be gleaned from the other. Giddens has emphasised that rights entail responsibilities—and this is symptomatic of 'third way' politics generally. But the analysis of Ericson et al raises a new concern, that responsibility is increasingly connected with 'choice' only in the narrowest of senses, and that it entails few rights outside the narrowest contractual ones.

[44] J Green, *Risk and Misfortune* (London, UCL Press, 1997).

It would be wrong to generalise from one study into the way that insurance operates. However, we should think back to the arguments in chapter 3 about the way that accident law might be reformed. In particular, the description of systematic deselection and 'unpooling' on the part of commercial insurers is one reason to doubt Patrick Atiyah's suggestion that first party insurance would be the best replacement for tort law. Although Atiyah makes reference to the virtues of self-reliance, it was suggested in chapter 3 that he is probably still aiming to achieve the twin goals of universal coverage and progressiveness which are the aspirations of social insurance in its familiar forms, with just a little political 'realism' thrown in. If so, he occupies the middle terrain, in which revelation about what the *technique* of insurance can lead us to achieve, collectively, seems to encourage a sense that the precise *form* of insurance, and its political context, are less important. It is still, as it were, a technique of security. But this is not necessarily the case, if institutions of insurance are becoming increasingly institutions of differentiation. We need to think carefully about what it would really mean to deal with accidents through first party insurance, by closer attention to the nature of insurance markets and other 'private' methods of providing security.

4. Conclusions and Comparisons

Individualisation is not only or even chiefly to be observed in respect of changes in insurance practice. There are currently many developments which threaten to undermine security and may be presented as 'individualising' processes. Sometimes these have been presented as simply unavoidable, posing challenges in the sense that institutions need to adapt. This is the essence of the 'Third Way' theories. According to Giddens, for example, social democrats must seek ways of responding to new conditions, and embrace the 'energising' element of risk while seeking to foster social inclusion. This tends to mean heavier emphasis on institutions which support individual, rather than universal, risk planning. At other times, individualisation has

153

been presented as a strategy, rather than an inevitable aspect of a changing global economy. In the hands of neo-liberals, it even appears that we should come to despise security, and to dismantle the existing systems of security in order to achieve an individualised route to satisfaction of social and economic goals. For many, the 'changed economic and social conditions' so quickly accepted by third way theorists are not an inevitability, the product of impersonal forces, but the net effect of neo-liberal ideas applied domestically in key economies, and internationally by key institutions.

Dworkin's egalitarian liberalism, and Giddens' attempt to spell out a social democratic vision of the 'third way', represent positive readings of individual responsibility and personal risk management. Both employ similar imagery of a bundle of resources, whose use over a lifetime should be planned by the individual resource-holder, or individual household. But the ways that this image are used are quite different, and the differences are instructive. In Dworkin's hands, the image spells out a hypothetical ideal, with such strong normative force that state institutions should model reality to resemble it. On one hand, this takes individualism extremely seriously as a normative matter. On the other, this is not 'individualisation': it assumes the possibility of state institutions taking whatever form is necessary, and (as explained above) Dworkin appears to assume the very kind of centralised and influential state institutions of risk management that are now argued by some to be ineffective. His model is the basis for a taxation plan. For Giddens, household planning with a bundle of resources is a solution to the kind of practical problems of economy and society which are not explored by Dworkin. Individual choice and individual planning in the response to life risks need to be supported by state institutions, but it is planning in the very imperfect reality of an increasingly insecure environment that Giddens has in mind. Individual responsibility is not so much an ethical or normative idea, as a consequence of change and a device to support the new solutions.

These are two very different positive readings of individual responsibility in the distribution of resources. But bubbling

154

beneath these two are more nightmarish readings of the same 'changed conditions'. For some commentators, such as Ericson et al, the 'individualisation' currently being experienced is one where narrow choice, but not freedom, is paramount, differentiation is the method, and surveillance is translated from the state to the private sector. For others, such as Bauman and Beck, the changed conditions of working and living bring about not freedom, but loss of security and enhanced responsibility.

The idea of risk as in any sense related to strategies for maintenance of security has in many contexts become increasingly associated with individualism and responsibility. An undercurrent to all of these developments is that whatever 'choices' we may be inclined to make, the responsibility to think in terms of risk is not one where there is any room for negotiation. In other words, the individual is neither as free nor as sovereign as may at first appear; or that 'sovereignty' is narrowly framed by the applicable methods. Perhaps it is true that people are becoming better at seeking out and receiving information, but the production of information in terms of risk continues and indeed accelerates. We may relate this to Bauman's observation regarding the effects of rapid change in the methods by which decisions need to be made, an effect which he describes in terms of 'uncertainty'. The *private* world he describes as 'essentially undecidable, uncontrollable, and hence *frightening*', adding that 'the present, already familiar frames of action will not remain constant long enough to allow a correct calculation of the effects of one's actions . . .'. Citing Doel and Clarke, he refers to the resulting atmosphere as one of 'ambient fear'.[45]

Such issues may help us to appreciate the link in Beck's work, which can appear problematic, between individualisation and the 'reflex' reaction to modern risks. For Beck, the individualisation brought about by changing risk issues does not stop where it is (institutionally) convenient for it to stop, but the individuals of risk society continue to ask sceptical questions about risk and about risk-benefit conclusions which they have

---

[45] Bauman, n 28 above, p 83.

previously been expected simply to accept. Individualisation is thus linked with the development of 'critical autonomy'. This in turn is relevant to understanding changes in the approach to risk assessment and evaluation in the effort to regulate hazards, which is the topic of the next chapter. Although exposure, insecurity, individualisation and even fear are relatively easily related to the undermining of expert risk assessment and decision-making, I will suggest that trying to close the door on such fears, and to achieve decision once their influence has been admitted, is much more problematic.

Part III. Environment, Precaution, and Sources of Change

6
Environmental Regulation, Risk, and Precaution

The environmental context has plainly been a particular testing ground for 'risk'. Here, hopes have historically been raised that statistically-based techniques can be used to guide decision-makers to objectively appropriate solutions; or at least to protect their decisions from criticism. On the other hand, this is also an area in which the limits of risk assessment have been clearly exposed. This makes it an especially useful place in which to explore sources of change in the kinds of decision-making method associated with 'risk'.

Through attention to these sources of change, which are also challenges to the decision-making methods associated with risk, we will be able to raise issues about societal decision-making and responsibility which develop the central themes of this book. Some of the challenges which emerge here are directed at the received methods of decision-making employing 'risk', particularly the interpretation of 'rational' decision-making and its precepts. These affect all aspects of decision-making invoking risk, including methods applied in making *individual* decisions. But their implications are particularly significant when we turn our attention to *societal* decision-making. Choices which are made through analysis of relevant environmental risks may be informed by statistical information relating to probabilities; but the direction of research into environmental decision-making in respect of risk has increasingly made plain that such decisions are indeed *choices*. Much discussion has surrounded the question of how to make such choices appropriately (whether this is taken to mean rationally, democratically, or in such a way as to build trust and avoid that which was not intended). But equally significant questions are thrown up concerning the sustainability of choices in the light of changes over time, and concerning the question of responsibility.

Strydom has recently emphasised that the language of risk, including risk analysis and 'risk assessment', was introduced into the environmental field predominantly by safety analysts. According to him, this constituted a first stage in the evolution of environmental risk discourse,[1] where the 'risk assessment debate' was an essentially expert debate. In Strydom's analysis, there has been a progressive broadening of the debate from these origins, resulting in increased political engagement with 'risk' issues on the part of the public. His analysis fits with our suggested evolution in risk, from a technical role in supplying statistical information and methodical expertise for the purposes of safety analysis, to the embrace of broader and more inclusive methods of decision-making.

In earlier chapters, it has been shown how risk, as a 'way of thinking', cannot be said to lead inexorably toward common solutions based on actuarialism and (perhaps) relatively 'empty' of moral judgment.[2] Rather, 'risk' has been increasingly associated with a focus on the individual, both in terms of choice and to some extent in terms of responsibility. Against this background, the environmental context appears to be distinctive because here, recognition of subjectivity, diversity, and even critical independence in respect of risk, has come hand in hand with increasing ambitions to achieve some sort of 'control' over hazard-creation. More than this however, in recent years such features of individual response to risk have also been treated as a potential resource in the construction of *public* decision-

---

[1] P Strydom, *Risk, Environment and Society,* (Buckingham, Open University Press, 2002) 15.

[2] Actuarial theories are not always empty of moral judgment. They have often built in arguments about 'fairness', especially in a distributive sense. See for example Ewald's suggestion, that the growth of actuarial method is associated with a new emphasis on distributive justice; and Atiyah's concern with the fair burden of paying for insurance.

making, perhaps as compatible with shared or collective responsibility. To some extent, we need to consider whether critical independence about risk, and public control, are indeed natural partners, or whether this is a new exercise in wishful thinking on the part of those who would like to see workable improvements in regulation of hazards while retaining trust and legitimacy.

Certainly, there seems to be a more positive approach to 'individualisation' where the environment is concerned. Recognising the role of individuals in negotiating risk, and particularly their emerging skills in recognising and resolving risk issues, has seemed to many to assist attempts to break a deadlock faced by expert or statistical approaches to risk. The difficulty is that diversity and independence in the recognition of risk and the formulation of solutions is not necessarily or at least easily compatible with resolution of the problems in question.

In the first section of this chapter, I concentrate on Quantitative Risk Assessment or 'QRA'. To some environmental lawyers, 'risk' is still synonymous with QRA, which is in turn often regarded as a purely scientific or numerical approach to risk-planning. I will look beneath the surface of QRA to explain how the 'quantifying' aspect of the technique always interacted with questions of acceptability and has been associated with a particular view about preferences. The more recent decline of any pretence that there could be a purely statistical form of QRA illustrates how approaches to risk acceptability—and particularly the reception of popular or lay responses regarding risk acceptability—have changed in recent years.

In the second section, I will isolate some separate roots for the currently changing approaches to risk, with attention to some very different, but nevertheless linked, theoretical sources. The first set of sources focuses on more or less internal doubts and questions raised about decision theory, and particularly about the role both of preference and of rationality. These developments help to form a bridge between questions of probability, and questions of democratic process, though on the whole they concentrate on decisions and the way that they are made. In questioning not only the rationality of behaviour, but also the

161

'untouchable' nature of preferences, these developments have contributed to the general shift in focus, to more collective approaches to *decision-making*. Notice that the idea of collective decision-making is very different from the idea of technical expertise used in conducting decision-making for collective ends.

The second set of theoretical sources is concerned with deliberative democracy, and particularly with the attempt to rise above pluralism and the preoccupation with preference, while remaining in a liberal tradition. It has clear overlaps with the first, though it is based on quite different concerns. The third source is identified through Hajer's 'reflexive ecological modernization'.[3] This approach seeks to harness the 'critical autonomy' of citizens, and does so within a framework of assumed mutual responsibility.

All of these move beyond the 'preference-based' approach to expected utility which was not only a hallmark of 'economic' risk methods, but which also had significant influence on liberal approaches to decision-making more broadly. Nevertheless, I argue that these approaches all continue to relate to the ideas we have identified throughout this book as concerned with 'risk', not only by default (they concern uncertain hazards, so that is their subject), but also in their methods to an important extent.

In the end, I suggest that revisions to decision-making techniques are inspired by a variety of different factors, and that these revisions aim at methods which are both more open about subjectivity and uncertainty, and more inclusive of different perspectives. But in some ways, these changes only make more obvious the limits to what risk methods can hope to achieve, while stressing their breadth and ubiquity. In particular, I will suggest that no matter how far we take 'improvements' to decision methods informed by risk, these decisions are still preoccupied above all with 'the present'. This develops a theme which was included from the early stages of our investigation of risk

[3] MA Hajer, *The Politics of Environmental Discourse: Ecological Modernization and the Policy Process* (Oxford, OUP, 1995) 279–94.

methods, namely that their main virtue is above all to enable decision-making. This leads us to the final section, which introduces some reflections on uncertainty, the future, and precaution.

1. From Expert Systems, to Value Systems? Risk Assessment, Risk Perception, and 'Acceptable Levels'

By contrast with the position in the US,[4] it would be misleading to suggest that UK environmental law has been centrally preoccupied with risk. However, risk assessment has often been debated, and risk 'methods', especially in their statistical guise, have appeared to provide useful tools particularly for the most familiar 'expert-dominated' methods of regulation. This section explains how developments in the understanding of risk and its acceptability have diluted the purely 'statistical' elements of risk, and at the same time weakened the hold of experts over judgments employing the methods of risk.

In particular, Quantitative Risk Assessment ('QRA') was an early candidate for inclusion as part of environmental policy-making. Acceptance of QRA for certain purposes by, in particular, the Health and Safety Executive was based partly on the recommendations of the Royal Society.[5] The use of QRA in

[4] Partly in the interests of 'transparency' and accountability–at least of the type that allows for and/or is able to withstand legal review–formal statements about risk levels are quite usual in the United States. For an account of new trends toward formal standard-setting in UK risk regulation, described as being based explicitly in a quest for accountability and a misplaced desire for objectivity, see E Fisher, 'Drowning by Numbers: Standard Setting in Risk Regulation and the Pursuit of Accountable Public Administration' (2000) 20 *Oxford Journal of Legal Studies* 109–30.

[5] Royal Society, *Risk Assessment: A Study Group Report* (London, 1983). Note that a second report followed, with the ambition of integrating some social and natural science approaches. It failed to do so, retaining instead a series of separate and unintegrated chapters. These Reports mark stages on the way to an increased recognition of legitimate controversy in risk assessment: The Royal Society, *Risk: Analysis, Perception and Management* (London, 1992).

developing formal standards helps to illustrate the link between a particular approach to risks, and the regulatory framework. It illustrates the impact of scientific expertise of a very specific kind.

QRA operates by ranking potential hazards according to the size or 'level' of the risk. This is typically expressed either in terms of the number of fatalities to be expected per (for example) million individuals in any given year, or by estimating the probability of a single individual dying in any given period of time as a result of the hazard. To this point then, QRA addresses the size of risks in terms of one common measure, and is not concerned with the benefits of the risk-creating activity. Hence, this form or aspect of risk assessment is heavily quantitative, in contrast with decision-making models which integrate the value of options. Thus, the technique can be used to show which hazards pose the greater risks, and to compare environmental risks with other 'accepted' hazards, in order to propose their acceptability.

There is significant controversy about this exercise. Occasionally there have been suggestions that existing levels of accepted risk might be used to propose the acceptability of new risks, on the basis that the new risk does not exceed a level which is already accepted for some other hazard.[6] QRA may be used in this way to introduce some 'perspective' into discussion, provided it is accepted that comparisons can only be made in order to propose acceptability where the risks being compared are broadly 'similar'. However, similarity in risks is itself a complex notion, and for the purposes of acceptability should be seen to comprise ideas such as the voluntariness or involuntariness of exposure; avoidability; and equity of exposure. But these are only initial points. The more serious objection is that size of risk cannot in itself, alone, indicate acceptability or unacceptability. We will return to this shortly.

[6] C Starr, 'Social Benefit versus Technological Risk' (1969) 165 *Science* 1232–38. See text accompanying n 12 below. Notice that even Starr considered that only relevantly 'similar' risks (in terms of the type of hazard and its voluntary or involuntary nature) should be compared.

QRA is influenced by an engineering approach.[7] According to Brian Wynne, risk assessment methods emerging from processes of design and manufacture operate within tightly controlled parameters in which problems are clearly defined and reliability is either testable or amenable to actuarial evidence.[8] In QRA, hazards are identified in terms of potential undesired outcomes, and probabilities are attached to these potential outcomes. QRA has clear potential for standard-setting, therefore, but use of risk in this particular formal sense has faded from the centre of recent environmental policy-making. This reflects broader trends in discussions of 'risk' as a whole, and charted in the present chapter.

There are a number of significant weaknesses with using the kinds of numbers produced by QRA as the basis of action. Most of the data regarding *familiar* risks (such as hazards in the home or on the roads) are based on statistical information of a broadly 'actuarial' kind: fatalities are experienced each year, and can be used fairly confidently, in most situations, as the basis for predictions relating to following years. But certain other risks, especially those relating to nuclear waste or new technologies, are much less amenable to calculation in the same way. These are precisely the sorts of risks that the public has been accused of overstating, at the expense of more familiar hazards. But the truth is that a quantification of the hazards posed by a new technology such as genetic modification of crops, or of low probability-high intensity risks such as those stemming from disposal of nuclear waste, requires a wholly different method. Past experience is no guide. Thus the figures for these risks must be constructed and understood very differently from the

[7] Royal Commission on Environmental Pollution (RCEP) 21st Report, *Setting Environmental Standards*, Cm 4053, 1998, ch 4, p 51.

[8] B Wynne, 'Uncertainty and Environmental Learning: Reconceiving Science and Policy in the Preventive Paradigm' (1992) 2 (2) *Global Environmental Change* 111; quoted by G McDonell, 'Risk Management, Reality and the Precautionary Principle: Coping with Decisions' in R Harding and E Fisher (eds), *Perspectives on the Precautionary Principle* (Sydney, Federation Press, 1999) 192.

experience-based figures for other risks. In this context, QRA methods become highly misleading.

Above all perhaps, where QRA concerns more 'uncertain' risks, whose quantification is not based on actuarial experience, there is legitimate concern about the estimates or quantifications *themselves*. These quantifications may be derived from a variety of methods including the construction of 'fault trees' and other devices. Thus those making the estimate must consider the ways in which damage may come about, and also the likelihood of those hypothetical problems. It has been argued that these methods are themselves beset by subjectivity and heavily influenced by the 'framing' techniques of their authors, so that the *approach* taken to cases of uncertainty may itself change the order of risk very significantly. As the Royal Commission on Environmental Pollution points out, grave underestimates of hazards of this type can stem in particular from over-optimism about the reliability of future expert systems in dealing with complex, untried problems.[9] This sort of over-optimism can become embedded within a professional context, and it has been argued that there is every reason to think that the biases affecting expert risk assessment are as systematic as those affecting lay responses.[10] But beyond this, there are legitimate variations in how uncertainty and indeed ignorance *themselves* affect the public consciousness.

At the extreme, the whole nature of what can be understood by 'risk' changes. Rather than being a question of what *number* of outcomes of a specified kind will occur, the question becomes one of imagining what the outcomes might be. There is a new question of whether or not a risk *exists*, and so the very first stage—of specifying the possible bad outcomes whose probability needs to be addressed—becomes highly significant, and politically highly charged.

[9] RCEP, n 7 above, p 54.

[10] P Slovic, *The Perception of Risk* (London, Earthscan, 2000) p xxxii, and ch 25, 'Trust, Emotion, Sex, Politics and Science: Surveying the Risk-assessment Battlefield' at p 390.

Nevertheless, QRA has been accepted as the basis of regulation in certain contexts, and there is occasional surprise that the method is rejected, or even that different levels are set for different hazards. Why is it that no consistent value is placed on a human life across very different hazards? But even to ask this question is to overlook many variables. For example, public responses to risk have been shown to depend not only on the size of the risk, but also on other less quantifiable factors such as voluntariness, equity in exposure/benefit, perceived worth of the activity which gives rise to the risk,[11] and the possibility (even if remote) of truly catastrophic loss of life if the worst scenario should arise. We could add to this a specific contemporary fear that the type of hazard may have longer lasting effects beyond the initial loss of life, for example through contamination of the gene pool, lasting effects on human intellect or fertility, or loss of biodiversity. None of these factors should be seen as irrelevant or irrational, and they feed into the idea of 'irreversibility', which is significant for its role as one of the conditions of 'precaution'. On the contrary, the richness of factors revealed by study of risk perception provides decisive reasons against deciding on risk acceptability using wholly statistical methods.

The truth is, where 'acceptable levels' have been used to inform regulation in the UK, these levels have always been variable as between different activities. It would be wrong to think that this is in any sense an exception to logic made necessary by the need to keep the public happy, for the reasons above. But increasingly, it is also suggested that acceptability is not merely a matter of probability combined with preference, but (rather) of reasoned debate aimed at designing best strategies. Though weakening the hold of *statistical* method, these developments do

[11] In support of my implication that the worth of an activity is not easy to quantify, there are two separate points: (a) There is often disagreement about the appropriate valuation; but also (b) no 'all-purpose' valuation exists, even for one individual, of given assets: their valuations depend on the circumstances and the reason for attaching the value. As to (b), see the discussion of logic of choice and psychology of value, below.

in a sense bring us closer to, not further from, the decision-making *spirit* of 'risk' which was proposed in chapter 2 as a key element in the appeal of risk to liberal theory.

Starr's 'Revealed Preference' Approach

QRA is not simply the product of a pure numerical approach to risk assessment, nor is it an entirely practical exercise in quantifying cause and effect through a process analogous to design and manufacture. One inspiration for QRA and even for some of the work disputing it is an early article by Chauncey Starr on how to achieve appropriate social trade-offs between safety and social benefits.[12] Acceptability, rather than merely expectancy value or quantification of risk, was a crucial component of this approach from the start. Starr is now often described as having taken a 'revealed preferences' approach.[13] Many of the social science approaches to risk perception seek to criticise Starr's work, but in doing so they also retain a focus on acceptability. It is interesting to note some prescient elements of his agenda, as well as those elements of it which have been superceded. We will spend some time considering these, because this will help us to identify some of the most distinctive changes in the way that risks have been approached in respect of hazard regulation in recent years.

Starr was seeking a method for tabulating both hazards (which he called 'risks'), *and* socially acceptable levels of exposure. His ambition was to inform a largely expert and numerical system for assessing risk acceptability, supported by relevant tables. Certainly that system should draw on the general social acceptability of risks, including the previous response of the public as a whole to similar hazards, and should not depend on a simple cost-benefit analysis prepared from an expert point of view. However, the goal was to enable decision-makers to determine *in advance* what level of risk was socially acceptable. Social

[12] C Starr, 'Social Benefit versus Technological Risk' (1969) 165 *Science* 1232–38.

[13] N Pidgeon, *et al*, 'Risk Perception' in Royal Society, *Risk: Analysis, Perception, Management* (London, 1992) 89.

acceptability was not treated as 'illogical' (*against* logic). It was however treated as effectively *beyond* logic, and at the same time broadly predictable.

In his ambition to enable *prospective* judgments to be made about the risks from new technologies, it is important to note some continuity between Starr's concerns, and the direction of some of the newest approaches to environmental regulation. In particular, Starr argued that we should seek *deliberately* to guide and regulate technical developments so as to achieve maximum social benefit at minimum social cost. This element of QRA has in fact been one of the more controversial, since it has seemed to many policy makers that the emphasis on deliberate acceptance of certain hazards should be moderated. In 1988, the Health and Safety Executive, for example, used the idea of 'tolerable' rather than 'acceptable' risk to cover all but the smallest of risks. For example, where nuclear installations were concerned, there should be efforts to reduce even tolerable risks to the lowest level reasonably practicable (captured as the 'ALARP' standard).[14] They should be progressively minimized, not fully accepted.

But the main contrast which Starr had in mind was between his preferred model of deliberate and prospective decision-making, and the existing 'empirical' process by which he argued that acceptable balances of benefits against social costs had in the past been identified, by trial and error. In a sense, this fits well with one element of Hajer's 'ecological modernization' (which he identifies as relatively newly-dominant in environmental discourse and policy), as shifting attention away from 'react-and-cure', towards 'anticipate-and-prevent'.[15] But it is not usually thought now that observation of the past can provide answers to the acceptability of *future* risks. Some of the reasons for this are explored later. More presciently perhaps, Starr also commented that 'we now face a general situation in which widespread use of a new technological development may occur

[14] RCEP, n 7 above, p 53.
[15] See the discussion of Hajer in sec 2(c) below.

before its social impact can be properly assessed'. This he attributed to social and economic factors, rather than to the pace of scientific discovery *per se*. But in the age (in particular) of genetic research, the attempt to have social assessment catch up with technical change appears to be an even more pressing issue. His approach nevertheless seems too optimistic in its attempt to reach a stable idea of acceptability, capable of being maintained over time.

The 'revealed preference' element of Starr's approach lay in the way that acceptability of existing risks could be gleaned from historical tracking of risk levels. If society could be seen to have responded to experienced risks by trying to reduce them over time, then the original scale of the risk was higher than acceptable. If however risks remain constant over time, then they must be of a generally acceptable level taking into account their benefits. This argument certainly lacks finesse, since Starr was vague about the mechanisms by which people were supposed to become aware of risks, and by which change was supposed to come about. On the other hand, by applying this rough and ready method, Starr was able to identify at least one major distinction, between the 'acceptable' levels of voluntary and involuntary risks. He thus acknowledged that most technological risks, with their involuntary nature to the majority of those exposed, would need to be much lower than voluntary risks if they were to be acceptable.

Similarly, Starr thought that the means by which the benefits of an activity could be assessed by the public generally would be significant, although he portrayed the public as broadly trusting of those who made social decisions, and highly responsive (for example) to advertising or public service campaigns. This may or may not have been a correct perception of public response at the time of Starr's writing.[16] But whatever the answer to that speculative question, current concerns with building public trust and with the variation of public from expert assessments of risk

---

[16] Strydom implies, to the contrary, that protest and doubt were in full swing by this stage, with an emphasis on nuclear protest.

are such that from no perspective is it likely that the public would now be portrayed in such a passive way. Indeed certain approaches now regard the public not only as being worth 'studying', but as being directly able to inform decision-making.

Generally, some of the most doubtful aspects of Starr's approach spring from his assumption that differences in the 'acceptable' level of various risks could be attributed to differences in the character of the risks themselves. As such, once risk acceptability was understood, relevant findings could be incorporated into a fairly technical form of decision-making. Public response would be an object of study, but the information gained would be used in creating tools for technical decision-making. Current trends, as described below, tend to take a far less 'tabulated' approach; they tend to approach the idea of 'values' as being distinct from 'preferences', whereas Starr treats these as interchangeable; and they treat decision-making as turning less on the nature of the hazard per se, and more on the whole context in which the decision takes place, including particularly the alternative options.

Transforming Risk Assessment

Growing appreciation of the limits of techniques such as QRA is capable of leading to a major transformation in the role of 'risk'. For example, the RCEP suggests that 'uncertainties' in risk assessments should be made clear. They should not be artificially hidden by building them in to the assessment itself, either through worst case scenarios or in some other way (such as attempted best estimates), since this is too misleading. Yet if this advice is heeded, any risk assessment produced for many of the most widely discussed hazards would need to take a discursive rather than a purely statistical form.[17] Such a change in the nature and presentation of risk would be enormously significant, since it would inevitably affect the extent to which conclusions

[17] The main difficulty perhaps is in reconciling this observation with the RCEP's own continued commitment to numerically expressed standards.

could be reached on the basis of mainly statistical information, or could be expressed in mainly quantitative form.

Risks, Options and Decisions

This leads us to a final observation in respect of the idea of acceptable risk. It is one which 'cuts both ways' so far as public participation is concerned. According to Fischhoff et al,[18] discussion of 'acceptable risks' is misleading in itself. There is no such thing as an acceptable risk. Rather, there are only acceptable *options* involving risks. The choice or decision of how to act is heavily dependent on what the alternatives are, as well as being dependent on evaluation of hazards and benefits.

This is in marked contrast with Starr's approach, which is also the general approach of QRA, where the nature of the hazard provides the relevant information enabling it to be ranked and its acceptability assessed. True, we need to ask what is gained by the activity which created the hazard. But also, could safer alternatives be designed? Could the activity be avoided altogether, or does the hazard-creating activity fulfil a need which only similarly risky activities could fulfil? Should risks be treated as part of a continuum with likely gains, or are they to be treated differently? In a sense, these questions provide yet another set of reasons why broader input is essential to the framing and resolution of risk issues.

But on the other hand, this certainly does not mean the end of 'risk' as a method of thinking and deciding; nor does it mean that the public's often fearful stance on technological risks can be imported unaltered into decision-making. On the contrary, by focusing on 'options' and alternatives Fischhoff et al reinforce, in its broadest outline, the decision-making paradigm associated with risk and central to decision theory, though they have questioned many of its applications and argued for an enriched and extended process for decision-making. Whether expressed in terms of 'choice' between options or chiefly in terms of 'decision', their approach emphasises that hazards can

---

[18] B Fischhoff, *et al*, *Acceptable Risk* (Cambridge, CUP, 1981).

neither be fully quantified, nor fully avoided. When members of the public cease to be mere 'objects of study', and become direct participants in decision-making, it is likely that their views will be more closely scrutinised and tested in certain respects. The lesson is that we have to learn to live with risk, not only in the sense of exposure to uncertain effects, but also in the sense of a way of thinking.

Some theorists now propose that the best escape from the stand-off between members of the public and experts of various kinds (policy-makers and both industry and government scientists among them) is to involve people more closely in the full decision-making process which goes to the framing and the resolution of risk issues. This is not only because something can be learnt from the contributions of the public, although this is certainly a strong part of the argument. It is also because this will encourage members of the public to reflect upon their attitude to risks and, ultimately, to be drawn into a process of decision-making that draws in some way upon the methods associated in this book with 'risk'. I will explain below why the emerging dominance of decision as a focus of study in relation to societal risk-taking reveals some important changes in the way that risk is approached. There are also changes in what it might mean to focus upon decisions. In particular, the focus on individual decision-makers which can be found in much economic theory has gradually been challenged by new approaches concerned with questions such as how to involve everyone in the process of group decision-making, and not only to 'deal with' diversity of view, but also to use it.

Even so, to engage the public in the act of decision-making under uncertainty is still to draw them in not only to a risk discourse, but also to a thought process in which benefits, hazards, and uncertainties must all be weighed. So while writings from a number of very different theoretical backgrounds could be seen as pointing the same way—giving more attention to public responses to risks, and less decisive weight to statistical accounts of risks and costs—they nevertheless do not weaken the dominance of risk discourse. They agree, in fact, on the necessity for devising a framework within which the activity of thinking not only about risks but also with the conceptual apparatus of risk—identifying problems, predicting effects, weighing and choosing options—can operate effectively.

2. Sources of Change

Recently then, we have seen some notable convergence into one broad set of recommendations (urging wider and more effective participation), from very different intellectual sources. This is striking enough in itself, but all the more so since it seems to contradict the trends in previous chapters, through an effort to reinstate common control and to bring people and government together in common decision-making, possibly even against the tide of economic or market reason. Yet in much of the work visited in chapter 5, economic and market reason seemed impossible to resist. Therefore, the same challenges of 'uncertainty' and the same doubts about probabilistic (or actuarial) solutions find a very different response in this context, as theorists seek ways of legitimising collective decisions and bolstering shared responsibility. Diversity here is not generally understood in terms of inevitable fragmentation. Whether we regard individuals as primarily 'sovereign' or 'critically autonomous', the question arises of how this can be positively reflected in the processes of decision-making.

(a) Logic of choice and psychology of value

Rational choice theory uses the terminology of 'risk' to refer to 'choice under uncertainty'. 'Uncertainty' for this purpose is generally the uncertainty of the roulette wheel: it need relate only to absence of knowledge about which outcome will follow, such as whether the gambler will win or lose the bet. It is generally capable of being addressed as a matter of probability, and no more far-reaching form of 'uncertainty' is implied. Theories of rational choice are used to comment on decisions about whether or not to run a risk, and whether it is worth spending additional sums on extra precautions.

Such approaches treat decisions about natural hazards as equivalent to gambles, at least in terms of the models applied to the choice of action. Thus they make use of the general idea of 'expectancy value' discussed in chapter 2 above, which is a combination of probability and utility, incorporating the idea of risk aversion. Above all, 'preferences' are thus treated as a key component of the decision, and rational methods are sought for maximising utility as measured according to these preferences. Decision-making is and should be a function of expected outcomes *and* of preferences among those outcomes.

There are many grounds on which the theoretical dominance of rational choice theories could be challenged when applied to societal risk-taking. For example, it may be argued that a collective decision, affecting many people, should not be made according to preferences alone, but should build in important elements of *equity*. Bad outcomes (if they follow) will be unequally suffered, and more likely than not they will be suffered by people who do not at the same time take the benefit. This kind of argument is sometimes supported by appeal to Rawlsian theory, or to more direct and less elaborate principles of equity.[19]

Importantly though, a significant body of work, instigated by Kahneman and Tversky's research into the psychology of decision-making, has begun to question not just the *application* of rational choice theory in more collective settings, but its very foundations even when applied to the central case of choice between gambles. Kahneman and Tversky ask hard questions about the very building blocks of established rational choice theory, derived from study of the same kind of decisions as were central to its development, namely personal gambles. Other writers have been instrumental in extending similar insights and

[19] For a discussion of Rawlsian theory, particularly maximin, see for example K Shrader-Frechette, *Risk and Rationality* (Berkeley, CA, University of California Press, 1991) ch 8. Less elaborately, see *Environmental Justice*, ESRC Global Environmental Change Programme Special Briefing No 7 (ESRC, 2001), illustrating how environmental impacts fall disproportionately on lower income groups even within the UK (globally, the picture is starker).

approaches to environmental hazards,[20] with lessons for social decision-making as to their regulation. This is one route by which a focus on decision-making in the round has developed.

Deviations from Rational Choice

Kahneman and Tversky's 'prospect theory' provides an alternative descriptive, rather than normative, account of the way that people actually make decisions. The results of their experiments into the psychology of decision-making propose that there is a sharp division between the descriptive and the normative dimensions, which rational choice theory has treated as identical. That is, rational choice and especially economic theory propose that people generally *are* rational maximisers of their preferences. But Kahneman and Tversky have provided ample evidence, mainly through laboratory study but with some increasing support from 'real life' contexts, that the choices people make are not consistent with the precepts of rational choice or economic theory.

On one level, this could be taken to mean simply that people often act *irrationally* instead, since they fail to recognise what course of action under uncertainty will best serve their interests. There is certainly an element of this. For example, Kahneman and Tversky illustrate how the 'framing' of the question by the questioner—the way that the issue was phrased—can be used to manipulate the responses of the individuals questioned. It is important to be aware that this is not only a feature of the response of lay people who are uneducated in the use of statistical probability. Doctors who were asked to choose between different treatments also fell into the same trap, as (often) do experienced investors in financial markets.[21] Nevertheless, the

---

[20] See particularly Paul Slovic, n 23 below.

[21] P Bernstein, *Against the Gods: the Remarkable Story of Risk* (New York, John Wiley and Sons) ch 16, 'The Failure of Invariance', 269. In addition, Daniel Kahneman has explained that the first subjects of the psychological 'experiments' involved in prospect theory were in fact Kahneman and Tversky themselves. It was initially their own wayward responses which were tracked and tested for consistency outside the dictates of economic rationality: D Kahneman,

implications of prospect theory go far beyond a discovery that human beings are not, on a regular basis, rational decision-makers.

Implications

For one thing, the wider significance of this simple point about deviations from rational behaviour should not be overlooked. Economic and rational choice theory *depend* upon the theory that people are rational maximisers of preferences, because the choices and actions of preference-holders provide the only real evidence of what those preferences are. The theory of rational choice is not accompanied by an account of the content of preferences any more than Starr's 'revealed preferences' approach was accompanied by a theory of what causes risks to be accepted. Preferences are simply an accepted mystery. Logic surrounds the choice of actions which will *maximise* preferences, but it does not lead us to question the formation of preferences themselves. Their content can be gleaned only by observation. If people are not acting and trading so as to maximise their preferences at all, then rational choice theory cannot identify these preferences, and cannot propose how to act. Rational choice theory *needs* the descriptive and normative levels to coincide.

An alternative is simply to ask people what their preferences are, rather than to observe their choices and thereby glean their preferences. The trouble is, there is again no useful way of *quantifying* preferences except by asking people to make hypothetical decisions or attach hypothetical prices. These processes would be as surrounded by the problems of framing and rationality failure as were real decisions. Indeed, Kahneman and Tversky's early experiments reveal precisely that this is the case. Furthermore, most attempts at eliciting preferences in this way are afflicted by a bewildering—and debilitating—lack of context. To be asked in the abstract what sum of money one would attach to aspects of the environment, or what sum one would

'Preface' in D Kahneman and A Tversky (eds), *Choices, Values and Frames* (Cambridge, CUP, 2000).

demand in payment for pollution of some aspect of it, is to be asked an impossible question. What, after all, are the alternative uses of the same sum of money? And how 'beneficial' is the activity causing the pollution? Is the pollution reversible? How much of the asset is left? Even so, this is the method adopted by contingent valuation methodology ('cvm') to value aspects of the environment such as air quality. Further insights into the failures of traditional notions of cvm have been provided by writers such as Slovic, and are discussed briefly below.

But the greater challenge to rational choice theory lies in the very regularity of the 'wayward' responses noted by Kahnemann and Tversky. Their descriptive theory has been able to say far more than just that people fail to act as 'rationality' would dictate. To select one particular issue, they have argued that the typical 'preference curve' needs revision, from the even curve proposed by rational choice theorists, to one which is steeper for losses than for gains. Threatened losses are avoided far more strenuously than potential gains are sought. Indeed, Kahnemann and Tversky referred to the property typifying human responses in decision-making as *loss* aversion, and distinguished this from risk aversion. They propose that people are reluctant to take the chance of losing assets they already have, yet happily engage in risky bets with an outside chance of securing gains—provided the price of the bet is low enough. This is why expressing a question in terms of likely losses or gains is likely to alter the responses gathered. Associated with this is 'endowment effect':[22] people will place a considerably higher sale price on something they already have, than they would be willing to pay for the same thing, if they did not own it. Traditional economic theory explains only much smaller disparities between an individual's buying and selling prices.

Also linked with these observations is a further implication of prospect theory. Rational choice and economic theory gen-

---

[22] Simply explained by D Kahneman, *ibid*, p xiii; and developed by R Thaler, 'Toward a Positive Theory of Consumer Choice' in D Kahneman and A Tversky (eds), *Choices, Values and Frames* (Cambridge, CUP, 2000) 269.

erally describe 'utility' as a property of states of wealth (that is, the eventual outcomes of risk taking). But prospect theory suggests that people who make decisions are far more concerned with *changes* in their states of wealth—with losses and gains—than they are with those states of wealth as such. If correct, this casts doubt on extensive use of mathematical expectancy value, which treats all sums of money (and all 'values' expressed in money terms) as equivalent. Furthermore, endowment effect, loss aversion, and association of utility with losses or gains could be used to help explain attitudes to environmental risk. There is reason to think that people will be wary of risking existing amenities in order to achieve potential future gains in terms of increased wealth or quality of life, and this could even help to explain some of the public wariness of modern technologies. Psychologically, people may not be so inclined to go for the 'glittering prize' of greater affluence, if they fear what might be lost.

Extensions

Such observations have been extended to apply to social questions. Paul Slovic, for example, has emphasised the doubt which must surround the very nature of 'preferences' when it is realised that preferences are frequently 'reversed' or revised depending on what question is asked, and even depending on the precise wording of the question. For example, people asked to rank the importance of air quality as opposed to an upgraded computer chose air quality as the more important. Yet the same people when asked to place a money price on the two assets attached the higher price to the upgraded computer, perhaps because they were more used to valuing assets of this sort in money terms. This is 'preference reversal'. It illustrates further why use of 'expressed' preferences (through processes such as cvm) is questionable. It is highly likely that rankings between assets will be unstable and contradictory.

Slovic's wider point though is that preference reversal is only one relevant phenomenon among many. He argues that judgments and preferences are not simply 'read off' some master list when an individual is asked to make a decision.[23] Rather, preferences are 'constructed' in the process of making the decision in question. Furthermore, people are very adaptive decision-makers who adopt a range of techniques in order to reach a decision. As Kahnemann has made clear, 'framing' is not only something done *to* decision-makers by the person designing the questions; it is also something done *by* decision-makers in order to assist decisions.[24] Slovic expressly suggests that techniques are sometimes oriented to avoidance of indecision—in other words, people like to reorder information in order to provide recognisable reasons for action, to allow clear decisions and *perhaps* also to avoid regret. This, I would suggest, is an important insight into the nature of decision-making. It has real implications for what can be achieved.

Accordingly, Slovic quotes Krantz's argument that individuals are not maximisers of preferences, nor indeed of anything at all. Rather, they are problem-solvers embracing a wide range of incommensurable values and with techniques at their disposal to make decisions between these in different circumstances. The problem to be resolved seems to be, with increasing study, the very question of *how* to decide. Decision-making itself thus becomes the focus. As Slovic argues, 'truth ultimately resides in the process, rather than in the outcome'.[25]

Slovic proposes that where valuation of the environment is concerned, cvm should be adapted in the light of this new focus on decision-making process rather than maximisation of outcome. He suggests that in complex questions such as those raised by cvm, it is important to take a deliberate approach to 'value construction', rather than sticking to simple preference elicitation. If, he argues, we focus on eliciting preferences, we may well find inconsistency and bizarre results. Perhaps we will

---

[23] P Slovic, 'The Construction of Preference' in Kahneman and Tversky, *ibid.,* 489.

[24] Kahneman, *ibid*, p xiv.

[25] Slovic, n 23 above, p 500.

even find that there is nothing to 'elicit' at all. Slovic suggests that the process of decision-making can therefore be designed in order to help 'value construction' to be performed 'rationally', and so that the final expression of values can be seen to be defensible. His approach only departs from more traditional preference elicitation to a certain extent. He emphasises the 'rational' aspects of value construction and decision theory, and continues to emphasise the guiding hand of decision-making agencies or 'experts'. Yet he also argues that decision-making is a highly contingent process, in which the answers will depend very greatly on the nature of the process adopted.

An important focus of Slovic's work then, which seems to mark a major departure from previous rational choice and perhaps revealed preference models, is that preferences are seen to be made rather than simply given. They are also hard to prioritise or list in any specific order. The 'preferences' which seem to motivate reactions and choices are constructed through the decision process, and generally not pre-ranked by the individuals who hold them. This is very significant, in that it links with the deliberative approaches below in its emphasis on the idea that values are capable of being constructed as part of a process around decision-making.

These extensions of prospect theory into a focus on societal decision-making supply an important link between the probabilistic/technical, and democratic accounts of responses to 'risk'. Some sources of the democratic account are further explored shortly below. For Slovic himself however, the focus is on the decision-making tactics employed by individuals in selecting their preferred option, and on the design of processes which will help this sort of process to operate more rationally. For proponents of deliberative democracy, the focus is on the political process of value-formation in one specific context, that of deliberation.

(b) Procedural approaches: deliberative democracy

By contrast with the 'decision theory' of Slovic and others, much writing on deliberative democracy has its theoretical roots in constitutional liberalism.[26] In its liberal constitutional forms, 'deliberative democracy' probably stems from a concern to get beyond pluralism.[27] It is concerned to rescue democracy from becoming an exercise in the mere satisfaction of preferences or negotiation of interests, while retaining its legitimacy as part of a broadly individualist philosophy. Given the particular problems with rendering environmental assets in 'preference' terms, this has made it especially interesting to environmental lawyers. At the same time, it retains the idea not only that pluralism of value is a fact but also that respect for individual choice or preference in some form is at the root of all legitimate collective action. Democratic process, on this view, allows for the coming together of parties in a particular public process which, properly conducted, is capable of being more than the sum of its parts. The process of democratic deliberation allows for the *transformation* of people's views. This goes further than the idea of preference construction arrived at by Slovic, though it is in a similar vein. The idea is that values themselves—rather than just the options which are thought to give best effect to them—are capable of revision through *debate*, including the idea of interaction with the views of others. For Slovic, values and preferences were predominantly constructed through the process of choice and decision-making.

At the same time, many proponents of deliberative democracy also argue that the public culture which arises from this process is valuable and healthy in itself. Hence, this aspect of liberal constitutional theory seeks to explain how a strong public culture, consisting of more than respect for individual values

[26] Having said that, the 'deliberative democracy' of John Dryzek is derived from a critical theoretical tradition influenced by Habermas rather than by liberalism. Dryzek has argued that insufficient attention has been given to the critical theoretical roots of deliberative democracy, and too much to the liberal side of its heritage. See J Dryzek, *Deliberative Democracy and Beyond: Liberals, Critics, Contestations* (Oxford, OUP, 2000); J Steele, 'Participation and Deliberation in Environmental Law: Exploring a Problem-Solving Approach' (2001) 2 *Oxford Journal of Legal Studies* 415–42.

[27] See for example J Bohman and W Rehg (eds), *Deliberative Democracy: Essays on Reason and Politics* (Cambridge, MA, MIT Press, 1997).

and preferences, is itself consistent with individual sovereignty. In environmental law, the idea of 'public values' has particularly been used to explain how laws which protect amenity interests or (by extension) values which are not of immediate economic importance to individuals, may nevertheless be a legitimate part of a liberal legal system. This provides a rather stronger justification for action than, say, cvm. Cvm sought to work out how individuals valued particular ecological assets. Because these were (by definition) the kinds of assets where people had little or no experience of exchange, the mechanism tended to founder when people were asked to make comparisons couched directly in money terms. Instead, this approach tends to ask people how they think that society as a whole should value certain things, including environmental assets.

As Mark Sagoff emphasised, the answer to these different questions may in turn be very different, even when supplied by the same individual.[28] Though some would argue that only money 'talks', and that hypothetical responses about social decisions should be disregarded, there are others who suggest that the distinct question of what sort of society we wish to be in is deserving of serious attention in itself, and that this can *only* be reached through discussion. Otherwise, a series of discrete exchanges with limited knowledge of the larger picture is likely to dictate the future: the future will be a matter of patterns which have been unplanned by anyone. Thus deliberative democracy defines itself in distinction from preference-based exchange values.

On the other hand, the idea of planning the future also suggests, implicitly, a distinction from the sort of 'side-effects' which according to Beck derive from the habitual under-estimation of hazards. Such effects are underestimated partly because of the existing processes and intellectual methods applied to the estimate of risks. But because the heritage of liberal versions of deliberative democracy is largely a background

[28] M Sagoff, 'Can Environmentalists be Liberals?' in M Sagoff (ed), *The Economy of the Earth* (Cambridge, CUP, 1988).

of liberal pluralism, this aspect of its potential is not fully articulated.

A number of significant questions arise regarding the application of deliberative democracy, and especially in the environmental context. Some of these are philosophical questions. For example, if the emphasis is on transformation through debate, and especially on the emergence of shared public values, then are there to be strict entry requirements concerning the types of interest one may bring to bear on one's arguments, or indeed the kinds of argument that are allowed? Will only a narrow and selective group of arguments and interests in the end be able to take part in the deliberations in question?[29] And how are 'public' values to emerge? Does 'consensus' need to be reached before decisions can be made? Philosophical questions arise about how such a consensus is in any sense possible given divisions of value and interest. Can such differences be stripped away by debate, and overcome through reason?

We have to leave aside these important philosophical issues, because our concern is not to test the theories but to note their method. We should also note however that there are also equally significant questions about the *application* of such ideas. One particular problem concerns the timing and the nature of such deliberations. Are they, for example, to be used principally in connection with specific decisions about whether to allow or to prohibit a proposed development? If so, then the application of deliberative forms of participation is likely to take the form of an unwieldy and expensive additional stage to the processes of decision-making. From the point of view of commercial and industry decision-makers, this will generally be resented. In some cases, years of research and development appear to be held up by a process of public consultation at the final stage. This could create an atmosphere of distrust, possibly even three way distrust, between public, agency, and industry. It is also inclined to enhance a feeling of adversarialism and opposed interests. The very idea that shared values will evolve through

[29] LM Sanders, 'Against Deliberation' [1997] *Political Theory* 347–76.

debate may be contradicted by employing deliberative processes in this way. Public values might end up struggling for influence against commercial or developmental interests. Still more seriously perhaps, there would be repercussions for the legitimacy of regulatory action, which was the very core concern of deliberative theory.

At their best, deliberative processes could lead to the questioning of received views and the emergence of a coherent series of public commitments. At their worst, they could simply raise confrontation without resolution. If we start with 'legitimacy' as our key concern, and worry above all about how to justify anything which departs from the interplay of personal preference, then this sort of problem will tend to be overlooked. An alternative approach derived from discourse theory has proposed the adoption of somewhat similar techniques on a different basis, and has urged that these can be used to add new dimensions to a strongly non-adversarial approach.

(c) Ecological modernization and democratization

The trends collectively described in terms of 'ecological modernization' take on board the practical challenges to traditional regulation visited immediately above. As described, influentially, by Hajer, ecological modernizers seek to minimize conflicts of interest and to emphasize the *benefits*, in all terms including economic ones, of environmental protection. Environmental protection thus becomes a 'positive sum game'. Ecological modernization is strong on integration. It seeks both to integrate economic and environmental interests, and to integrate ecological issues into economic decision-making. The rhetoric of ecological modernization minimizes the attention given to conflicts of interest, seeking to emphasise the degree to which the environment is a 'public good' and the extent to which the economy may be strengthened by ecologically prudent activity.

It is a natural and even inherent aspect of ecological modernization that agenda-setting and problem-identification should be proactive and prospective, not reactive, and that ecological problems should be considered in an anticipatory way, in order

that environmental impacts should be integrated into all decision-making. Ecological modernization is therefore concerned
with changing the techniques of regulation and indeed with the
reorientation of decision-making in general. It tends to facilitate
coalitions of interest and reduction of conflict. In this as in much
else it is reminiscent of 'third way' approaches. It has a strong
but not unconditional 'fit' with the needs and logic of a market
economy. On the other hand, it requires that governments act in
order to integrate ecological thinking into the logic of market
decision-making. The integration of ecological concern to market thinking and the proposed stimulus to technological innova-
tion in pollution prevention will not occur spontaneously, but
only through governmental action. Principles such as 'polluter
pays', prevention, and 'precaution' are regarded as inherent
aspects of ecological modernization, for example. So are cost-
benefit and risk-benefit analysis, techniques which seek to make
the environment count in economic terms. The discourse of
ecological modernization encourages the perception of shared
problems with solutions that can be appreciated as such by all.

   The general method of Hajer's work is not to champion economic modernization, but to observe and chart its development.
Importantly, his primary concern is to underline the importance
of discourse in ecological politics, and the influence of discourse
coalitions in environmental policy. The rise of ecological politics
as a whole on Hajer's account owes much to the emergence of
these discourse coalitions. Though members differ in their
motives and in many of the detailed elements of their intentions,
these discourse coalitions maintain certain 'story-lines' concerning, for example, the depletion of the ozone layer or destruction
of the rainforests. Sustainable development, according to Hajer,
is one such story-line, created by and in turn helping to maintain a *global* discourse coalition. As Hajer notes, this coalition
'can only be kept together by virtue of its rather vague story-
lines at the same time as it asks for radical social change'.[30] Thus
Hajer's thesis is to a large degree sceptical of existing ecological

[30] Hajer, n 3 above, p 14.

politics, asking what exactly the problems are perceived to be, and denying the validity of beginning with realist definitions of the ecological problems.[31]

But the detachment of Hajer's stance is not unlimited. Finally, he also wishes to propose institutional changes for improved policy formation. In particular, he emphasises the potential benefits of participatory elements for the future of ecological modernization. Here he argues that certain changes in the agenda will be required in order to bring about his preferred 'reflexive' form of modernization.[32] The nature of his solution, and the *type* of problem it is thought to resolve, are our main concerns here.

The 'reflexive' version of ecological modernization contrasts with existing forms, which Hajer considers to have a 'techno-corporatist' bias.[33] In improving upon these, he implies that new models will contribute to the ideal of a democratic process of *deliberate* social choice.[34] This process attaches not only to particular issues and courses of action, but also to larger-scale scenarios of 'development', and to social visions or plans of action. This is an attempt at prospectivity and anticipation which avoids 'last stage' confrontation. For Hajer, the exchange of views should not take place at the end of a planning process, as in litigation, but much earlier. The creativity of rival views and projects should thus be used, not lost. Disagreement is (somehow) to be resolved into answers to the broadest questions, about how to orient our actions. Hajer is explicit that we need to avoid unwanted social 'side-effects' and, instead, plan developments with effects that are intended and deliberate.[35] Importantly, we should 'put an end to mediocre naturalist environmentalism', and seek more explicit reflection on 'the sort of development society really wants'.[36]

[31] *Ibid*, pp 13, 16.

[32] 'Reflexiveness' he gives a discursive meaning, unlike Beck's meaning of a 'reflex' of self-confrontation.

[33] Hajer, n 3 above, p 281.

[34] *Ibid*, p 280.

[35] *Ibid*, p 283.

[36] Loc. cit.

We should note the centrality, in Hajer's thesis, of this contrast between social 'side-effects', and the sort of development that is 'really' wanted. Hajer makes plain that the search for 'deliberate' decisions is an essential and defining element in his proposed 'reflexive' form of modernization. 'Reflexive institutional arrangements', he explains, are formats 'that facilitate deliberate decision-making in the age of risk society'.[37] It will be noted that the context of these decisions, as taking place 'in the age of risk society', is also of defining importance. Yet the idea of being 'deliberate' in the context of risk and uncertainty is exceedingly problematic. Hajer touches on the difficulties that arise here, but in the end downplays them.[38]

Hajer proposes that the best route to deliberate and planned choice as to the future lies not in a narrowly technical analysis of likely risks and outcomes, but in a form of consideration where the debate is opened to non-specialist points of view. This may take the form of scientific interdisciplinarity, and does not imply the abandonment of science or specific disciplinary skills. But more centrally, Hajer suggests (building on Beck's work) that what is needed is the 'mobilization of independent opinions'.[39] Where deliberative democracy regarded individual preferences and values as sovereign, and needed a way of devising public action that respected this, Hajer's 'reflexive ecological modernization' seeks improvement to decision-making, through inclusive debate.

In arguing for greater participation, Hajer aims to release the power of different understandings of the world and 'different sorts of knowledge'. Citing Beck, he argues that greater enlightenment will follow if the grasp of scientific rationality and expert authority is loosened. In the past, these methods broke taboos and advanced enlightenment. At present however, they hinder

[37] Hajer, n 3 above, p 286.

[38] Through a reference to work by Keller and Poferl. Hajer concludes that the issue resembles one of throwing out the baby with the bath-water (*ibid*, p 285), so that the problems of risk should not detain us.

[39] *Ibid*, p 282.

the process of enlightenment.[40] Exclusive methods are restrict-ing, and this certainly includes the methods that we have come to recognise as involved with risk assessment. Rather, decisions should be as broadly informed as possible.

This approach gives significant emphasis to the process of decision-making, and it devolves certain responsibilities to participants in debate. Such participants must, in this context collectively, weigh possibilities and probabilities in order to determine which course of action best suits their purpose. The insight that traditional forms of risk assessment have hidden cer-tain hazards, and that broad reflection is needed both in relation to risk definition and in respect of final decisions, does not alter the fact that people are thus drawn into the language and spirit of decision-making according to 'risk'. They must model the likely outcomes of action and select the best options accordingly, in recognition of the uncertainties involved.

I suggest that Hajer's argument that broader debate, freed from the dominance of single-subject specialisms, will lead to a more deliberate approach to development and its environmental costs, presumes strongly risk-based thinking, despite building in scepticism about judgments based solely on probability or statistics. Indeed scepticism about the possibility of purely methodical or expert solutions to the question of how to act is likely to strengthen the need for all participants to think more directly, on their own account, in broadly risk-based terms. How, if at all, can decisions be regarded as fully 'deliberate', the goal that Hajer proposes? By ensuring that the various options have been set out, costed, and planned, *and* that the continuing risks associated with them have been accepted. This latter addi-tion, of the acceptance of risks, is essential, given that 'side-effects' are to be avoided, and given Hajer's own specific location of these processes against the backdrop of 'risk society'.

---

[40] Loc cit. It is important not to assume that 'science' in the abstract demands clear and objective answers and is therefore inherently obstructive to the kinds of solutions being discussed. More likely is that the reception and interpretation of scientific 'evidence' has become institutionalised to seek more finality than is appropriately claimed by scientific methods.

Putting it broadly, Hajer's approach suggests that all participants must grasp the nettle of what they want. This must include not only a sense of which things they value, but also an understanding of what they are willing to sacrifice in order to attain these. We saw in the context of Dworkin's insurance experiment that these were central aspects of responsible decision-making interpreted as risk-taking. Hajer's proponents too are required to be responsible risk-takers. Unlike Dworkin, Hajer does not use the language of responsibility and does not reflect on the nature of the responsibility that, with hindsight, will follow decisions. But in deploying critical opinion to open the black boxes of expert decision-making and lay bare the processes by which decisions are made,[41] reflexive ecological modernization also requires that participants think through the process of decision-making for themselves.

In the end, there are further formidable problems with designing reflexive institutional arrangements, and attaining 'deliberate' decision-making in the age, if not of 'risk society', then at least of contemporary risks. And the key undermining problem is surely one of uncertainty. The plausibility of Hajer's solutions depends in part on what sort of 'side-effects' he is keen to avoid, and what kinds of success he thinks can be achieved through such developments. Possibly, his true preoccupation in this respect is not with outcomes, but with the process of risk-taking itself. If so, the 'side-effects' in question will be not so much materialised risk (the consequences we hope to avoid), but the social effects of decision-making itself. In other words, the concern may be the relatively static one, in temporal terms, of building trust and confidence. I would say that this is also a question of building confidence in the kinds of risks that are collectively taken.

The difficulty is that this shared confidence, even if it can be attained, may be difficult to sustain over time, as the *outcomes* of development decisions—or what is identified as their outcomes—make themselves felt. The idea of deliberate develop-

[41] Loc cit.

ment, which is also bound to be deliberate risk-taking, is constantly threatened by the awareness of uncertainty. Uncertainty is far-reaching and beginning to take on new guises. That is one reason why we must consider its representation via the principle of precaution in what follows.

As methods, clear risk assessment and appropriate risk management may above all appeal to the conscience of the present, providing immediate absolution. Their ability to provide us with future forgiveness depends on the extent to which appropriate decision-making is seen as allowing us to escape responsibility for effects. We have already seen that in moral terms, this has not been thought to be the case. Lack of blame in the methods applied to decision or to action does not remove the sense of responsibility for outcomes. The sense of responsibility is extended to responsibility for dealing with unlucky outcomes, should they occur. But this effect is if anything growing as the sufficiency and robustness of formal decision methods is increasingly in doubt. The limits of even the most open and methodical approach are more clearly appreciated. Knowledge of this must in turn impact upon the conscience of the present, and on the ability to act. It must introduce an element, not just of uncertainty, but of doubt.

Appropriately extended and made inclusive, deliberative, and reflexive, decision-making methods may (in a more practical sense) help resolve the issues of mistrust and disagreement which confront present decision-making. But we know already that we will not be content if our gambles turn out badly. That is why we hold insurance to cover our gambles when it is available and affordable; and that is why 'outcome responsibility' (in Honoré's sense) imagined a repeat pattern of gambles in which we all mostly won. We are adding here that the comfort provided by the methods of risk is limited. As Hajer notes, insurance and compensation frequently fail, and this is particularly recognised in the context of modern ecological risks. Philippopoulos-Mihalopoulos explains the same phenomenon in terms of an ambiguity in the acceptance of risks: 'even if one accepts risk, one is hardly ever ready to accept its materialisation

. . . underneath our reluctant 'yes' there lies an ever-sonorous 'no'.'[42] This has large implications for the view we take with hindsight; but realisation of this has implications for the conscience of those making decisions now.

The problems here do not only concern foreseen possibilities, but also the chance that unforeseen side-effects of action will emerge. Hajer's 'reflexivity' may broaden the range of what we foresee, while reducing our confidence in which outcome is most likely. But in addition, human action will continue to have effects which are multiple and hard to track. No amount of anticipation can allow us prior knowledge of all such effects. To use the terminology of Ian Hacking's analysis,[43] we know that 'interference effects' will continue to arise—that one thing we do will interact with other actions to produce effects that have not been anticipated by laboratory studies nor by 'fault tree' methodology. But, crucially, we do not know what these effects will be. Increasingly, we know that declarations of safety are unreliable and falsely conclusive, but however clearly we acknowledge this, we still cannot anticipate all of the many potential effects of action. The future may be planned from here; but its shape will surely defy planning. Hajer's discussion of reflexivity and the pursuit of *deliberate* forms of development invites broader discussion about risk and uncertainty and, in particular, the *implications* of uncertainty for the idea of deliberate decision-making.

3. Uncertainty and Precaution

'Where there are threats of serious or irreversible damage, lack of full scientific certainty shall not be used as a reason for post-

---

[42] A Philippopoulos-Mihalopoulos, 'The Silence of the Sirens: Environmental Risk and the Precautionary Principle' (1999) 10 *Law and Critique* 175, 178.

[43] I Hacking, 'Culpable Ignorance of Interference Effects' in D MacLean (ed), *Values at Risk* (Totowa, Rowan and Allenheld, 1986).

poning cost-effective measures to prevent environmental degradation'.[44]

So far in this chapter, 'uncertainty' in its most challenging senses has been bubbling under the surface. It was one of the factors that made QRA a limited device for the resolution of risk acceptability questions, and it was raised again as an issue for any 'intentional' approach to environmental protection. It is sometimes assumed that the 'problem' of how to deal with uncertainty will be resolved, or at least the approach to uncertainty will be decisively altered, if the 'precautionary principle' is accepted as the norm in responding to environmental hazard. Since Hajer also lists the precautionary principle as an inherent aspect of 'ecological modernization' alongside other broad principles such as 'polluter pays' and 'prevention', it is important to consider whether the mysteries of uncertainty in its more far-reaching senses are capable of being 'settled' by such a principle. Furthermore, we can now add the question of whether we might be better able to think and plan in the *light* of uncertainty, given the emergence of this principle.

The answer is that precaution does not *resolve* the problems associated with uncertainty because in some senses it merely draws attention to them. Precaution certainly implies that lack of certainty should not be hidden, which is an aspect of the discussions above about the limits of QRA and which underlies the convergence of many views in favour of broad-based and participatory decision-making. It also recognises the fact that many effects can be established only after the event. In order to satisfy the requirements of 'proof', it may take many years to get from the supposition of potential damage to establishing a definite link between cause and effect. In its emphasis upon 'irreversible' damage (as well as serious damage generally), the precautionary principle recognises that not all risks and benefits can be treated as direct equivalents—as though they will cancel out in the long

[44] This particular statement of a precautionary approach is contained in Principle 15 of the Rio Declaration. There are many possible alternative formulations, but this is perhaps the best-known. See for examples Harding and Fisher (n 8 above), Appendix 1.

term, with careful decision-making. Some things, the principle seems to imply, are too important to be left to traditional risk assessment.

Supporters of the precautionary principle in one form or another often regard it as essentially linked with a participatory and pluralistic approach to governing.[45] The very idea of precaution, as briefly encapsulated in the extract from the Rio Declaration above, is perhaps incompatible with a purely expert-driven model of risk assessment, since it throws the issue of uncertainty beyond the reach of probabilistic representation. Others however suggest that it implies that new variants of the required 'burden of proof' might be formulated to justify either action or inaction, or they suggest a revised version of risk assessment to take due account of uncertainty.[46] But if we see precaution as truly embedded within a changing approach to governing, as O'Riordan and Hajer both do, then we may decide that precaution implies both less, and more, than a change in the burden of 'proof'. Apart from emphasising that ordinary risk assessment on the basis of the best available evidence will not always be sufficient, what does the precautionary principle actually require that we should *do*?

Action or Veto?

For lawyers, it is perhaps natural to see precaution as inherently to do with 'veto' over actions which might otherwise be taken—for example, as a ground for judicial review.[47] The strongest version of the precautionary principle might, it is argued, be precisely one that operates as a veto, by reversing the burden of proof. On this view, the principle is concerned firstly with the

[45] See for example T O'Riordan, Foreword to *The Precautionary Principle in the 20th Century: Late Lessons from Early Warnings* (London, Earthscan, 2002).

[46] D Pearce, 'The Precautionary Principle and Economic Analysis' in T O'Riordan and J Cameron (eds), *Interpreting the Precautionary Principle* (London, Earthscan, 1994).

[47] See E Fisher, 'Is the Precautionary Principle Justiciable? [2001] *Journal of Environmental Law* 315–34.

identification of doubt. After that, then it is clear that safety should be prioritised—whatever the costs.

But this kind of uncompromising approach to precaution is unlikely to succeed in attaining legitimacy or support, and in some respects it is not internally coherent. It is true that there are individual instances of specifically focused and discrete 'precautionary principles' in which there is a reversed burden of proof: the proposer must show that no harm will be caused (for example, to the marine environment) by the proposed action.[48] Thus there are individual instances of precaution operating as a veto. But these instances are best regarded as mini-principles with specific application. One of the difficulties with seeing precaution as a veto in terms of a *general* principle is that the dichotomy between safe and risky actions is false. This is the question of internal coherence referred to above. For example, less dumping at sea will mean more dumping on land, unless there is positive action to discover what else can be done with waste. Such a mini-principle is likely to be the product of broader thinking, and in many instances will require that precaution has already informed some *positive* steps. To put precaution first, and to try to compel some positive ideas towards a solution, is possible, but it would be a high-risk strategy indeed. It may also be incompatible with the implicit idea that safety must be preferred. Does a 'safe' route exist?

It has also been suggested that too 'negative' a principle of precaution (by which is meant, one which is concerned primarily with preventing action) is likely to fall foul of what has been called the principle of 'Reverse Risk Assessment',[49] according to which problems with no solutions are simply ignored. It is therefore argued that, all things considered, a precautionary approach is likely to be most successful if it seeks solutions, rather than

[48] Examples include the Oslo Commission statement on dumping of industrial wastes in the North Sea, 1989 (Harding and Fisher, n 8 above, p 305).

[49] D Fleming, 'The Economics of Taking Care: An Evaluation of the Precautionary Principle' in D Freestone and E Hey (eds), *The Precautionary Principle and International Law: the Challenge of Implementation* (The Hague, Kluwer, 1996).

simply rejecting action—particularly where that action currently provides benefits.

Equally, a 'negative' precautionary principle is likely to operate in a fairly uncoordinated way, in which the simplest cases are resolved first, not the most difficult ones. Thus, Fleming argues that a 'positive' approach to precaution as a *principle of action* ought to involve an exercise in prioritisation, in which the more dangerous or threatening issues are prioritised for action. In a way, this approach attempts to 'rescue' decidability in the face of uncertainty, and its recognition in the idea of precaution. This would appear compatible with Hajer's ideal of 'societal enquiries', in which there is widespread consultation and debate over which issues should be given attention in order for action to be pursued. It is true that this approach blends 'precaution' together with other principles, such as prevention. But perhaps this is the best way to see precaution: not as a single principle marking a clean break from preceding approaches to risks and hazards, but as part of the larger group of ideas marking a more 'intentional' approach to risks.

Precaution, Governmental Ethos, and Science

This section on the precautionary principle was introduced with a comment about the treatment of 'precaution' as one of a range of principles implicated in 'ecological modernization'. This would be hard to reconcile with the 'win-win' ethos of ecological modernization if the principle of precaution was really associated with reversed burdens of proof and with vetoes over action. But Hajer's treatment of precaution illustrates a particular European understanding of the principle, influenced by the nature of the precautionary principle (*Vorsorgeprinzip*) in its Germanic origins.[50] In particular, the German principle of precaution does not stand alone but is balanced by a number of

[50] The 'precautionary principle' is derived from the German *Vorsorgeprinzip*. This is certainly no reason to interpret the emerging international principle slavishly in accordance with its German origins, but the German context is interesting in its own right.

other principles, including particularly an idea that there should be proportionality in cost and gain.

In general, the precautionary principle in Germany is presented by both Boehmer-Christiansen[51] and von Moltke[52] as a powerful ally of government action, and as providing the opportunity for mutually beneficial results, even against the opposition of the economic sector. The language of shared interest is harder to resist than other regulatory-legal discourse, and has tended to draw in reluctant parties. *Vorsorgeprinzip* requires positive action both in terms of an integrated and 'comprehensive' research effort to identify potential dangers, and in terms of incentives for technological development which will lessen the environmental burden. According to this line of thinking, 'precaution' broadens the policy agenda by opening up more areas for action, even where scientific evidence is inconclusive. According to some of its opponents, it therefore gives too much emphasis to society-wide understandings of risk and benefit, and has insufficient respect for the understandings of particular (for example industry) preferences. But the whole objective is to arrive at workable and mutually acceptable approaches to potential dangers. The idea is that investment should prospectively *include* investment in environmental protection.

In its origins, the precautionary principle is therefore not identical to an approach requiring that we should 'put safety first', or give the benefit of the doubt to those who claim controversially to be 'exposed to risk'. It rests on more complex sentiments concerning a method of governance and of positive action. In particular, it seeks to give legitimacy to state action on the basis of active prospective planning.

The potential importance of the precautionary principle does not stop here. Especially important, it has been argued, is its impact on the status of 'science'. Some have argued that it

[51] S Boehmer-Christiansen, 'The Precautionary Principle in Germany–Enabling Government' in O'Riordan and Cameron, n 46 above.

[52] K von Moltke, 'The Relationship Between Policy, Science, Technology, Economics and Law in the Implementation of the Precautionary Principle' in Freestone and Hey, n 49 above.

marginalises science.[53] But in fact the precautionary principle depends upon science, and marks if anything a departure from the 'unscientific' habit of assuming that scientific claims are claims to certainty. On the other hand, it may also be true that the precautionary principle is one of the factors driving science into new and more openly argumentative modes.

Precaution and Responsibility

But the precautionary principle is also a very important focus for philosophical reflection. It suggests limits to risk assessment, which derive partly from the untested nature of contemporary risks and the absence of 'experience' on which to base statistical representation of these risks; and partly on the strong separation between these risks, and phenomena which can truly be regarded as matters of chance. In chapter 2 above, reference was made to the idea that the world is increasingly treated as a laboratory. I added that it was therefore increasingly unlike a lottery.[54] 'Precaution' captures the same sort of idea. The instigation of a 'precautionary principle', no matter whether it is essentially positive or negative, and no matter what the obstacles to its realisation, removes the comfort of aggregation and probability, and makes us focus again on the responsibility associated with action, and especially with decision-making.[55]

Through the idea of 'irreversibility' in particular, the precautionary principle asks us to recognise that our decisions, if they turn out badly, will not simply cancel out in the long run or over a number of repeat performances; and that this must be taken into account no matter whether the potential ill-effects threaten us as decision-makers, or indeed threaten future generations who as yet have no part to play in the decision. Simply, the pre-

---

[53] See S Dovers and J Handmer, 'Ignorance, Sustainability, and the Precautionary Principle', p 167, in Harding and Fisher, n 8 above.

[54] Ch 2, p 31.

[55] In U Beck, *The Brave New World of Work* (Oxford, Polity, 2000), Beck describes (at p 71) precaution in terms that supply an opposing force to the 'energising' effect of risk mentioned by Giddens. It is associated with moratoria and undecidability.

cautionary principle enhances the responsibility of decision-makers at the time of decision, and suggests that we should not let 'hope'—the continuing supposition that things may go well, or the denial of risk referred to by Philippopoulos-Mihalopoulos—dominate our thinking. Nor should we assume that an application of *sound processes of risk assessment*, on the basis of best available evidence, is sufficient to discharge responsibility. But the principle cannot tell us what exactly should be done in the light of this enhanced responsibility, nor even how precisely it should influence our decisions, except that we should no longer depend simply upon established scientific evidence relating to hazards.

As has been highlighted before in this book, increased awareness of the limits to statistical methods and especially of aggregating approaches has tended to be met by a new emphasis on responsibility, especially on the responsibility and choices of particular agents. In the environmental context where the precautionary principle is most applicable, the emphasis is increasingly on collective responsibility rather than on individual choices, but it is equally distant from 'aggregation'. In common with the problems faced by *individual* decision-makers, this new focus on responsibility appears to leave us adrift, facing all the choices and responsibilities which have been associated with risk, possibly even obliged to live our lives according to the precepts of risk planning, but finding its methods increasingly inconclusive.

Part IV. Conclusion

7
Reflections

Risk has been chiefly addressed here as associated with decision-making. We began by noting that even to name undesired potential outcomes in terms of risk is to begin to structure an approach to action. By extension, the language of risk has also been used by legal theorists to explain connections between action, and outcomes. Their theories incorporate ideas about chance and luck, rather than statistical probability, though these are sometimes addressed in an over-confident and too limited fashion.[1] We noted that the intuitive connections made by legal theorists between risk and action are more than superficial, but that they are under particular strain given recognition of more contemporary variations of uncertainty.

We also reviewed the central conceptual place occupied by risk in certain accounts of the evolution of welfare states. Here, risk is perceived as having a significant technical role: it provides a technique or set of techniques for controlling chance and its effects on the population. Insurance, with which risk is closely associated on these accounts, is a particularly significant development. But the technical dimension is not the only one that counts. The same developments have also been described as having an influence on the idea of justice, in the sense particularly of a just division. Indeed Ewald suggested that insurance lies beneath the change in focus from just attributions of responsibility, to just divisions.

Some liberal accounts of just divisions also employ risk but in a different way. Employing 'risk' has allowed these theorists to

[1] For example, certain issues treated as problematic within philosophical theories about moral luck were treated as essentially unproblematic within Honoré's theory of outcome responsibility.

deploy the element of individual choice in explaining the proper extent and limits of aspects of welfare. Dworkin's approach exemplifies a point made in Chapter 4, where I suggested that those liberal theories of liability for outcomes which express themselves in terms of risk are artificially limited if they do not pursue the question of insurance as an aspect of responsibility. His account showed less concern with the origins of solidarity, and with the ways in which political support for distributive mechanisms could be built. Indeed it gave little attention to vital supply-side questions concerning the process by which risks may be pooled.

Subsequently, we noted that aggregation was itself challenged by new developments in the handling of risk and welfare. For example, differentiation in insurance markets is claimed to be an emerging trend; and greater emphasis is placed on individual responsibility for anticipating and avoiding (or taking) risks. But although such developments appear to share with liberal legal theory an emphasis on individual responsibility, on reflection this is not the same idea. We contrasted the liberal idea of sovereign individuals who take responsibility for their own choices and in doing so are responsible for the setting of values, with the neo-liberal individual who has the responsibility for planning their life in the context of numerous uncertainties. Neo-liberal and third way ideas are partly inspired by the failure of collective solutions, whereas liberal theories continued to envisage a strong centralised state in order to deliver the just solutions arrived at by hypothetical individual decision-making. These latter theories employ a kind of moral and *hypothetical* responsibility for one's own choices,[2] in contrast with the real responsibility to plan and make provision to be found in third way approaches. If a less hypothetical responsibility survives real-world conditions on these liberal approaches, it is the responsibility to live collectively and to appreciate the limits of one's own claim to resources in the light both of chance and luck, and of the claims of others.

[2] In other words, this moral responsibility requires ideal conditions and can be only hypothetical in the real, non-ideal world.

Similar points can be made about liberal variants of deliberative democracy. These were among the diverse approaches visited in chapter 6, all of which developed ideas of risk and decision-making in ways that pointed towards the need to strengthen more collective forms of decision-making. At the same time, each of these approaches accepted the growing importance of individuals *in* collective decision-making, given the insufficiency of more narrowly statistical or quantitative approaches.

Like the theories of justice to which they are typically related, individuals in liberal approaches to deliberative democracy are perceived as *sovereign* in respect of value-formation. This time however the emphasis is typically upon a prospective contribution to public decision-making and the adoption of new decision-making strategies. These approaches therefore provide a liberal antidote to individualistic rational decision-making. Like the other developments in chapter 6, they may appear to run against other contemporary trends, which point towards disaggregation and greater individualisation, in that they press for a stronger public realm. I explained in chapter 6 that such approaches generally require compromises to be made by individuals, and that these compromises are compatible with the understanding of possibilities and opportunities in terms of risk.

In partial contrast, reflexive ecological modernization proposed better routes to reaching decisions, in which the individual contribution is perceived slightly differently. 'Critical opinions' are mobilised in order to clarify the options available; but in the end it is vital that individual opinion should not fail in the light of the difficulties facing any decision about risk. At the end of chapter 5, we referred to Bauman's image of 'ambient fear' where the methods of decision are subject to rapid change and where received methods have been progressively undermined. We could say that it is individuals, and the public itself, which have taken on the guise of a *deus ex machina* in resolution of risk questions. Public agencies are increasingly employed in the presentation of *information* on risks, all of which is conceded to be inconclusive. Decisions are deferred to the level of individual choice; collective decisions are presented in terms of preferred options. But to assume that people can play the part assigned to them in emerging decision-making models and be comfortable with risk in the fullest sense is to assume not only that they can approach decisions with the right spirit of independence and compromise, but also that they can be at peace with the sense of continuing exposure to hazards which will follow any decision.

This in turn touches on a significant theme, concerning the future. In addressing both responsibility for outcomes and distributive justice, liberal theory tended to make the fit between forward-looking and retrospective vantage points too comfortable. Indeed in some instances of legal theory, it was assumed that the idea of taking a risk, and shouldering outcomes, was so familiar and unproblematic that its very reiteration could help to justify responsibility for outcomes in moral terms and at law. I explained in part II of this book that the idea of risk-taking cannot in itself justify institutionalised outcome responsibility at the expense of, say, insurance solutions. Insurance, should it work, would be a better way of enabling action in the face of consequences, and is capable of being at least as fair. This makes it all the more significant that we now operate increasingly 'beyond the insurance limit'.[3] But this problem does not only face insurance-based approaches. The very same developments make the idea of individual responsibility for outcomes still more problematic, since outcomes become less familiar and predictable; responsibility potentially more far-reaching with continued exploration of causal links.

As a result, the word 'risk' refers to a method which is certainly not in decline but on the contrary, increasingly ubiquitous. At the same time risk is also often identified with a sense of continuing exposure to hazard or to potential bad outcomes. It is if anything increasingly common to require an analysis of situations in terms

[3] U Beck, M Chalmers (tr), 'Risk Society and the Provident State' in S Lash, B Szerszynski and B Wynne (eds), *Risk, Environment and Modernity: Towards a New Ecology* (London, Sage, 1996) 31.

of risk, or in terms derived from the methods of risk. But we have to recognise that to do this is not to close the issues. 'Problem closure' is an objective of, for example, reflexive ecological modernization. But it is a temporary phenomenon. I suggested that proposals for achieving better decision-making are largely oriented to the acquiescence of the present, not necessarily to better outcomes nor to sustained agreement. In evidence for this, the effects and interactions which follow human action are continually monitored, and the conclusions of these exercises will continue to be debated in their turn. At the same time, as advice on the basis of risk becomes more sophisticated and more transparent, it also becomes notably less conclusive. The precautionary principle, which asks us to prioritise safety, can itself be said to lead to ambiguity. To be competent in the methods of risk is, increasingly, to negotiate ambiguous and incomplete information and to exercise choice in the face of these.

The comfortable fit between liberal legal theory in many of its aspects, and theory of risk, has rarely been noticed even though there are many instances where legal theorists present their analyses in terms of risk. I have suggested that the use made of 'risk' within legal theory is more than superficial, and certainly goes beyond a mere question of terminology. But at the same time as uncovering and charting this relationship, I have suggested that the very comfort of this fit needs to be tested and questioned. In particular, many issues surround the relationship between decision and outcome, and therefore responsibility. Risk is not a comfortable and familiar emblem for responsible action, as it is sometimes treated; nor a narrowly statistical idea that can resolve problems by rendering them in technical and non-evaluative terms. In neither way can it be treated as shorthand for easy solutions to problems of responsibility. Indeed, bound up with risk are some highly problematic questions of responsibility, and some of the greatest emerging challenges to existing responsibility models. The precautionary principle and its ambiguities, particularly its implication of increased awareness of unacceptable potential outcomes beyond the reach of clear foresight and of loss-spreading, are indicative of this.

Index

Index

Index

Index

Index